In civilization, if one wants a board, one buys it from a sawyer.

I had to cut down a tree and saw or chop my own boards, which took a great deal of time and effort. Using these, plus such scrap lumber as washed ashore from the wreck, I extended my shelves all along the left side of my cave. I perfected my table and chair, which gave me a comfortable place to eat, keep my journal, and read . . .

As the new year of 1660 approached, I tried to look ahead rather than backward. I had much to do and learn.

A Background Note about *Robinson Crusoe*

Although *Robinson Crusoe* was published nearly 300 years ago, it continues to be an influential novel. The story of a man cast away on an island, forced to depend upon his own ingenuity, faith, and luck, seized the reading public's imagination and has never let go. The book has inspired countless imitators, ranging from the serious (including the 1812 novel *Swiss Family Robinson*), to less-than-serious movies with titles such as *Robinson Crusoe on Mars* and *Robinson Crusoe of Clipper Island*. The still-popular old TV sitcom *Gilligan's Island* and the 2000 Tom Hanks movie *Cast Away* also owe their inspiration to this timeless adventure story.

ROBINSON CRUSOE

◙ DANIEL DEFOE ◙

Edited, and with an Afterword,
by Jonathan Kelley

 THE TOWNSEND LIBRARY

ROBINSON CRUSOE

TP THE TOWNSEND LIBRARY

For more titles in the Townsend Library,
visit our website: **www.townsendpress.com**

ISBN-13: 978-1-59194-068-5
ISBN-10: 1-59194-068-0

Library of Congress Control Number:
2006926041

Contents

CHAPTER 1

Start in Life

I was born the youngest of three sons in 1632, in York, England. My father was an industrious German immigrant named Kreutznauer; my mother came from the prominent Robinson family. Following English custom, "Kreutznauer" became shortened to "Crusoe." My eldest brother was killed in battle against the Spaniards near Dunkirk. I never learned my second brother's fate, just as my parents never learned mine.

By the time I arrived, my father had made enough money to retire from business. I remember him as old and wise. He groomed me to study law, but I had a wandering spirit. I wanted only to go to sea. Father strongly objected; my mother and friends all implored me not to. Even at that stage of life, I seemed destined to disregard all good advice and take a self-destructive path.

One day Father made a determined attempt to talk some sense into me. His tone was kind and reasonable. Why, other than youthful impulse, would I want to leave my family and native land? I had been born with advantages; if I worked hard in England, I might enjoy a comfortable, successful life. Adventures, he said, were for two types of men: desperate men with no hope at home, and great men in search of fame. I was neither, and I should be grateful, for life had taught him that this middle station was the safest and best. I would suffer neither the endless toil of the poor, nor the worrisome sorrows that come with riches and fame.

If I heeded his words, he promised to help me find my way in life; if I did not, my suffering would be my own fault. He wept as he spoke of my oldest brother, with whom he'd had the same sort of discussion years ago. He had risen to the rank of lieutenant colonel—only to die in combat. My father said he would always pray for me, but that if I took this foolish step, God would not bless me. I would regret at length what I had decided in haste, with no one around to help me out of trouble. With that, which in light of later events was quite prophetic, he grew too sad to continue the discussion.

I was deeply moved—how could I not be? My initial reaction—to take his advice and stay—wore off after a few days. To avoid another discussion like that, I resolved to run away, but not before trying some persuasion of my own. I waited until my mother was in a good mood, then took her aside. I was determined to see the world, I told her, and would accept no less, so my father had better not try to force me to stay. If he did, I would run away; the same if he placed me as a law apprentice. But if she would ask my father to consent to one voyage, and I found it not to my taste, I would come home and work doubly hard to make up for lost time.

Agitated, my mother flatly refused. My father would never agree to something that was against my best interests, nor would she lobby him to do so. How could I even think of such a thing after the kind, loving way he had sat me down? I would never be able to say that she had connived in any way at my ruin.

Though she refused to make my case to him, I did hear afterwards that she reported the discussion to him, and that Father said to her with a sigh: "That boy might be happy if he would stay at home. If he goes abroad, he will be the most miserable wretch ever born. I will never agree to that."

Nearly a year passed with no solution. My father proposed numerous ways to get me started in business, but I remained deaf. Instead, I complained that my parents didn't understand or care what I wanted out of life. One day I was down by the port in Hull, with no particular plans, when I met a friend about to sail to London in his father's ship. Would I like to come along? I didn't even send word to my parents. It was an ill hour on the 1st of September, 1651, that I boarded a ship bound for London.

I doubt any young adventurer's misfortunes ever began sooner than mine. The moment we were out to sea, the wind and seas began to rise. I became miserably seasick. Perhaps it had been an awful mistake, and this was God's penalty for my careless disobedience. Thinking of my father's tears and my mother's pleas, I was as sad as I was ill. Later in life—in fact, very soon—I would see much worse conditions at sea, but right then it was the worst I knew. I expected every wave to swallow us up. I made a desperate vow: if God would spare my life, and I ever set foot on land again, I would go directly home to my father, take his advice, and never again go to sea.

These wise and sober thoughts continued while the storm lasted, and indeed some time after. The next day the wind abated and the sea calmed, and I felt better if not fully recovered. By evening all was quite calm, and the next morning the sun rose on a smooth, beautiful sea with a gentle wind. It was the loveliest thing I'd ever seen. I had slept well, my sickness had passed, and I was in excellent spirits. What had been violent was now peaceful. I might have acted on all my vows, but my friend came to me that afternoon.

"Well, Bob," said he, clapping me upon the shoulder, "how're you doing? That bit of wind last night frightened you, didn't it?"

"Bit of wind?" I asked. "What a terrible storm!"

"A storm? You fool, do you call that a storm? It was nothing. Give us a good ship, and we think nothing of such piddling weather. But you're a freshwater sailor. Let's make a bowl of punch, and we'll forget about all that and enjoy the day."

The short truth is that, like many sailors, I had a little too much punch. It drowned all my repentances and resolutions, no matter how hard they tried to return. I began calling them "fits," and did my best to shake them off. After five or six days of good weather I had overcome (or drenched) just about all of my own good sense.

As it turned out, God wasn't done with my lessons. If I wouldn't take a hint, the next one would be so powerful it would put my shipmates into similar "fits."

On our sixth day at sea there was too little wind to sail; we anchored off Yarmouth Roads to wait out the calm. A great many other ships also came to anchor and await a helpful wind, either to go upriver or out to sea. In hindsight, we ought to have worked our way to a more sheltered anchorage upriver. After four or five days, the wind came up, but too strong and not favorable to our destination. No one worried then; but on the eighth day, the wind grew so powerful we had to take down all sail and ride it out. By noon the sea was coming over the side; fearing for our anchor cable, we dropped a second. I watched both cables pulled full length, hard as long iron bars with the ship's entire weight straining against them.

Even the hardened seamen began to look afraid, but the worst was still to come. One time, as I was going on deck, I passed the captain and heard him say softly to himself: "Lord have mercy! We'll all be lost!" I spent most of my time in my cabin, unsure what to think. I could hardly go back and remake the vows I'd already violated. Through the spray of the sea I could see that two nearby ships had cut away their masts. My comrades cried out that another ship a mile ahead of us was foundering. Two more were completely dismasted, their anchor cables snapped, blown out to sea to their fates. Only the lighter ships could do anything more than hunch down and hope.

Toward evening, the mate and boatswain begged the captain to let them cut away the foremast. He was very unwilling, but the boatswain insisted that it was our only hope. At length the captain agreed. When they had sawed away the foremast, the mainmast stood so loose it too had to come down. Our decks were clear. The storm's fury grew, and even the old sailors said they had never seen worse; now and then one cried out that we might "founder." Good thing for me I didn't know what that meant, but I did know that the captain, boatswain, and a few of the more sensible hands were actively praying. That frightened me even worse.

Around midnight, a man came up from the hold crying that we had sprung a leak and taken on four feet of water. All hands were called to the pump. My heart sank and I went to my cabin, where the men quickly intruded on my despair. "You're not much use on deck, but you can pump as well as another," said the boatswain, escorting me below. Glad to be able to do something useful, I worked heartily.

While I was helping at the pumps, I heard a cannon shot topside. I later learned that the captain had simply fired a distress signal to a couple of passing coal haulers, but right then I thought the ship had broken, or some other calamity had done us in. I was overcome by the stress and I fainted away. Most likely someone just pushed me aside with his foot and took my place, thinking me dead. Who could be bothered to care about my situation, with every man in fear for his life?

It took me a long time to come around. When I did, I saw that the pumpers were losing the struggle. The ship would indeed "founder," said the men, even though the storm eased a little. The captain continued to fire guns for help, and a light ship that had just ridden out the worst of the storm sent a boat over to help us. This was very hazardous and brave of them, for the rescue boat was in great peril as it neared our towering side. We directed them astern, which was a bit safer, and cast them a rope. We must abandon ship.

Soon we were crowding into the rescue boat. With all of us aboard, the rescuers could not possibly return to their own ship, so the captain asked the boat's coxswain to take us as near shore as he could. If the boat were damaged in the process, he would reimburse her owner. This agreed, our overloaded little craft pulled for shore.

Barely fifteen minutes out of our ship, we saw its bow dip under the waves. "She's a-foundering!" cried one crewman; at least then I knew what it meant. My heart sank, not merely for our plight but for my own ethical miseries. This seemed a very stiff penalty for going back on one's vows.

But soon we could see the shore, and a great many people running along the coast preparing to help us. Our first steps onto dry land were an immense relief. We walked to Yarmouth town, where we were most kindly treated. The town magistrates assigned us good lodging, and generous merchants collected money to enable us either to return to Hull or go on to London, as we might wish.

Had I the sense to go home, I would have been the topic of a joyful celebration, for my father had heard that my ship was lost off Yarmouth Roads. As it happened, it would be a great while before he would learn that I had survived.

My ill fate pushed me on now with irresistible stubbornness. I don't know what to call this impulse, unless it would be "foolishness."

I didn't see the captain and his son until two or three days after we reached Yarmouth. When they saw me, they looked very downcast. Son explained to father that I had come on the voyage only as a trial, meaning to go further abroad. The captain turned to me and spoke in a grave tone. "Young man, take it from me: never go to sea again. You aren't meant for it."

"Why, sir," said I, "do you plan to abandon the sea yourself?"

"That's different," said he, "for it's my profession and duty. In your case it was a trial, and you can see Heaven's answer. Perhaps you brought this bad fortune upon us, like Jonah. What are you, and why did you go to sea?" I told him some of my story, and he burst out in laughter. "Where did I sin, that such an unlucky wretch should come aboard my ship? I wouldn't go on shipboard with you again for a thousand pounds. Go back to your father, and tempt fate no more. If you do not, you will see his words proven true."

I said little, and we parted soon after. I never saw either again. But now that I had a little money in my pocket, I traveled by land to London, where I continued to agonize over my future. What if I did return? My father might embrace me, but my neighbors would laugh and be smug. Youthful pride is a powerful force. I was not ashamed to sin, but I was ashamed of the effects of repentance, and in the end I made up my mind.

I was looking out for another voyage.

CHAPTER 2

Slavery and Escape

While my impulsiveness would one day lead me to disaster, for the moment I was having a brief period of prosperity. I wandered the London docks and taverns until I met a sea captain planning a second voyage to western Africa, known as the Gold Coast. When I said I was interested in seeing the world, he offered me free passage as his messmate and friend. If I could afford any trade goods, I was welcome to do some business.

Happily, I had been writing to some of my relatives, and they sent me some money. I suspect some of it actually came from my father—or, more likely, my mother. Perhaps they were too glad to hear of my survival to stay angry with me; in any case, I set off for the Gold Coast with about £40 worth of trade items.

On our way south, the captain took time to teach me shipboard and navigation skills. He was a man of deep integrity and skill, and enjoyed giving instruction. Thanks to a few fortunate stopovers, I was able to sell all my goods, taking payment in gold dust. When I returned to London, this brought me almost £300 in solid British coinage. As it turned out, I had made just enough money to ruin myself, but I certainly didn't feel like ruin then.

The voyage was not all joy. I was continually sick from the ship's motion and the extremely hot climate, for our destination was just north of the Equator—a long way from London. To make matters worse, my friend died soon after our prosperous return to England, leaving command of the ship to his first mate. Inspired by the promise of the Gold Coast trade, I embarked with him for a second voyage. I brought almost £100 with me, entrusting the rest to my friend's widow, and we sailed again for Africa.

We would indeed reach Africa, but neither the part nor in the way we wished.

On our way down the coast, not far north of the Canary Islands, a Moorish pirate appeared on the horizon in the early morning. He was rigged for a chase rather than a fight, so we tried to run for it with all sail. When it became obvious that we would be overtaken in a few hours, the new captain ordered us cleared for action. Our twelve guns were loaded and run out for battle. We counted eighteen guns on the pirate, but with luck and skill we might prevail.

About three in the afternoon he caught up with us, but with sailing ships, the pursued ship that swings around to fire a broadside usually gains an advantage. So it was here; our cannons roared, and he changed direction after an ineffective return broadside and an equally futile barrage of musket shots. Not a man of us was hit.

The pirate swung around to resume the attack, and this time he got close enough to board us. Sixty desperate men leaped and swung onto our decks, and began hacking at the rigging (and us). Armed with cutlasses, pistols, and muskets, we drove off this wave, only to receive a second and a third. In the end, we had to surrender our disabled ship. Three of our men were killed and eight wounded. All survivors were carried into the Moorish port of Sallee to whatever dreadful fate might await.

The rest fared worse than I did, I believe, for they were carried up the coast to the Emperor of Morocco's court, but the pirate captain saw my youth and kept me as a slave. From prosperous merchant to human property: my father seemed like a prophet. That said, I was not mistreated, and my situation could have been worse—as life, in due course, would be sure to teach me.

My new master took me to his estate as a servant. I held out hope he might take me back to sea again, where a Spanish or Portuguese warship might capture the raider and set me free. No such luck, for he left me on shore to tend his garden and do menial work while he was at sea. Once he returned, he ordered me to stay in his cabin aboard ship and watch his goods. I spent all my time thinking of a way to escape. None of the crew spoke English; I spoke no Arabic or Turkish. In this way I passed two years of dreary captivity without a single promising opportunity for freedom.

Things began to look up when my owner started going out in the ship's launch. He liked to fish, and began to take me along to row the boat and help him catch fish, for I was good at both. He was not pirating as much; the gossip said that he was short on money to fit out his ship. For whatever reason, these fishing trips became at least weekly excursions. They filled my mind with thoughts of escape, but there was always someone else along—evidently his trust in me was limited.

One calm morning we were out fishing when a thick fog rolled in very suddenly. Though we were only a couple miles from shore, we lost sight of it, and rowed all day and all night without knowing our heading. The next morning, we found that we had gone somewhat out to sea and must row further to reach shore. Though the wind came up pretty fresh, and we were tired and hungry, we made our way in.

In case such a thing happened again, the pirate captain ordered the captured longboat from our English ship fitted out with a cabin, compass, and provisions. He modified its rigging to improve its handling. Now we began to fish in this boat, which was easier work all around. It also improved my chances.

One day he planned to take two or three important men, also Moors, out on a fishing trip with us. For this reason he had a larger store of food and drink loaded aboard the previous night. He also ordered me also to pack three guns with powder and shot, in case his guests saw any interesting game to shoot at. I took special care in preparing the longboat, for one never knew when opportunity might knock.

The next morning my master came on board, and told me his guests had been delayed by some important business. They would dine at his house. I was to take Ismail, a Moor, and the boy Xury, a young Arab slave, and catch fish for this meal.

A little ship of my own, my master gone: what an opportunity! I had no idea where I should go, nor did I care. I needed a reason to load the boat up with proper provisions, so I had a word with Ismail. "We mustn't eat our patron's fine food," I explained to him. He agreed and loaded the boat with a large basket of ship's biscuit and three jars of fresh water. I swiped some bottles from the captain's stock of captured rum. While Ismail was ashore on some errand I put them in the cabin, along with a great lump of beeswax, some twine, a hatchet, a saw, and a hammer. The guns and ammunition were already aboard, and we three sailed out to fish, with Ismail suspecting nothing.

The people in the fort that guarded the harbor mouth recognized our boat and paid no attention, and about a mile out we hauled in our sail and started fishing. The wind was not ideal for me, for it blew from north-northeast—a southerly wind would have carried me to the coast of Spain, and at least the port of Cadiz. But I didn't really care; I just wanted out of slavery.

I fished as ineptly as possible, and Ismail had no luck. After catching nothing for some time, I told him: "This won't do. We'll have to move farther out, or we'll disappoint our master." He agreed, so we sailed a couple of miles out to sea. Then I gave Xury the helm, bent down near Ismail as though picking up something, and hove my Moorish companion over the side.

He was taken completely by surprise. He bobbed to the surface and begged: "In the name of Allah, let me back aboard! I will go all over the world with you!"

Ismail was a strong swimmer, but I was afraid to let him back, so I grabbed a musket from the cabin and pointed it at him. "You haven't harmed

me, and I don't want to hurt you, but I mean to be free. You swim well enough to reach the shore; I won't shoot you unless you try and get back aboard our boat. Now go." Ismail turned for shore, and I expect he reached it with ease.

I could have taken Ismail and drowned Xury instead, but I didn't trust the older man. When Ismail was receding from sight, I turned to the boy. "Xury, if you will be faithful to me, I'll make you a great man. However, you must swear by your father's beard and the beard of Mohammed to be faithful to me; otherwise I have to throw you overboard." He smiled, stroked his chin where a beard would someday grow, and swore good faith.

While Ismail was still in view, I took the boat

directly out to sea. With luck, he would report that I was headed for the Straits of Gibraltar, as any sensible person would have done. No one would expect us to go southward, where powerful Negro tribes dominated the coast with canoes and little love for intruders. Where there were no people, dangerous beasts prowled very close to shore. Thus, at dusk I changed our course to southwest, keeping in sight of land.

A fresh gale of wind enabled us to make excellent time. By afternoon the next day, we must have been a hundred and fifty miles south of Sallee. We were quite out of the Emperor's domains, but I took no chances. Five more days we sailed southwest along the coast of Africa, until I was nearly sure my former owner would have given up looking for me. The wind shifted southward, and we needed to go ashore for water. When we saw a stream mouth, we turned our craft landward.

I meant to wait for nightfall, but with night came such dreadful noises from the jungle that Xury begged me to wait for morning. "Very well, Xury," said I, "but by day we may see men as dangerous as whatever animals those are."

"Then we give them the shoot gun," said Xury, laughing, "make them run wey." This was the fractured English spoken among the slaves. I was glad to see the boy so cheerful; we dropped anchor and tried to sleep, but couldn't.

Two or three hours later we saw some sort of great creatures splashing down to the seashore, wallowing and washing and howling and yelling. I had never heard the like. Both of us were terrified, and more so when one of the mighty creatures came swimming over toward our boat. Xury thought it was a lion, and wanted me to hoist anchor and sail away, but there wasn't time and I didn't want to cut the cable. Instead I got a gun from the cabin and fired at the creature. Whatever it was, it turned back for shore.

The noise continued all night. By morning the splashing creatures were gone, but we could still hear howls and cries from the nearby forest. I wasn't eager to take chances, but who knew when we might find another water source? Xury offered to go on shore with one of the jars and get some from the stream. "Why should you go and not me?" I asked him, for I had grown to like him.

"If wild mans come, they kill me, you go wey," he answered.

For that, I couldn't let him risk himself alone. "Well, Xury," said I, "we will both go. If the 'wild mans' come, we will kill them before they kill us." We hauled the boat as near shore as we thought safe, took loaded guns and empty jars, and began to wade ashore.

On shore, Xury headed a bit upstream into the jungle where the water might be fresher. I kept the boat in sight in case any canoes showed up. Soon I heard a gunshot, and Xury came running back. I ran forward to help him, in case he was in danger, but he had better news: he had shot a large rabbitlike creature. Better still, he had found good fresh water, and seen no "wild mans." We feasted on the game and filled our jars, then prepared to continue south.

Based on my previous voyage through this region, I thought we might be near the Canary Islands, or perhaps even the Cape Verde Islands far south of them. Without instruments or charts, I couldn't be sure, but if we kept moving down the coast we would surely reach the Gold Coast region where Englishmen traded. This particular part of northwestern Africa lay forsaken, for the Moroccan emperor hardly needed any more barren country to rule, and the Negroes of Africa had far better options for living space. Only the beasts came here.

Once or twice in the daytime I thought I saw the peaks of Tenerife in the Canaries, but the wind was against us and the sea too high, so we kept moving. Several times I was obliged to land for fresh water, and early one morning we anchored just off a high point of land for this purpose. "Look!" cried Xury, who was paying better attention than I. "A monster sleeping on shore!"

It was a lion, lying in the shade of a small cliff. "Xury," I said, "go ashore and kill him."

He looked frightened. "Me kill? He eat me at one mouth!" He was probably right, so I took our biggest gun and loaded it with two slugs, then loaded two more with similarly heavy charges. These would have much shorter range, but would deliver the heavy blows necessary to harm the great creature. Shouldering all three weapons, I waded quietly ashore.

The lion didn't stir from his sleep, fortunately, and when I was close enough I put the first gun to my shoulder and fired. I was aiming for the head, but he moved just as the *boom!* of my weapon broke the morning calm. The slugs hit his foreleg, breaking the bone, and the monster growled and tried to rise. At first he fell on his broken leg, and with a terrible roar of fury he got up on three legs to have revenge. While he did so, I fired my second shot, and this time I hit the great head. The lion fell to the ground struggling for life. Xury took heart and wanted to go ashore and finish the job. "Then go," I said, and he came ashore with a gun in his hand. The lion did not react to Xury's approach, and a single shot to his ear finished him off.

This was game, but no food, and I was very sorry to have wasted three charges of powder and shot on it. Xury tried to cut the head off with a hatchet, but it was too large and mangled, so he settled for a great forepaw. I thought we might benefit from the skin, and with the boy's help I got it stretched out atop our cabin. If nothing else, it would be comfortable to lie on.

We could be doing better, but at least we were safe and free. Whether we could stay that way remained to be seen.

CHAPTER 3

Wrecked on a Desert Island

*A*fter this stop we continued south, eating sparingly and going ashore only for water. I wished to reach Africa's western extreme, a point called Cape Verde, which all European trading ships plying this coast must pass. If I could not reach that point, I would either have to try for the Cape Verde Islands or take my very slim chances with the coastal tribes, who had too often been plundered by slavers to have any great love for Europeans. I had no choice but to pin all my hopes on meeting with some ship at Cape Verde.

About ten or twelve days after the lion episode, I began to see people watching us from the shore. One time we came in relatively near view of a mixed group: men, women, and children, all Negroes, wearing very little by European standards. I wanted to go ashore to meet them, but Xury objected: "No go, no go."

"They aren't armed, Xury. Perhaps we can talk with them." He disagreed, pointing out one strong-looking native. This man was carrying a lance, and had the look of a man who knew how to use it. Their manner did not seem aggressive or hostile, however, so I hauled us in perhaps fifty yards away from them. Then I began to use the sign language I had learned as a Gold Coast trader.

They made the gestures for peaceful intent. I returned these, then asked if we could get some food from them. Yes, they signed, if I would stop my boat, they would bring me some meat. I lowered my sail and waited, and in a half hour they returned with some dried meat and grain—of what type we neither knew nor cared. Yet how could we accept the gift? I would not go ashore, nor did they seem willing to wade out to us, as our sign conversation made clear. Eventually the Negroes solved the dilemma by laying the food on shore, going a good distance away while we collected it, then returning.

We made signs of thanks to them, but for the moment we had nothing to offer in return. Then nature placed a means of payback directly into my hands, for two mighty spotted cats came sprinting out of the hills toward the sea. Perhaps they were the same sort I drove off before.

There was no way to know why the predators were in a hurry, but the Negroes certainly feared the worst. All the women and most of the men retreated. The lance-bearer stood his ground with calm courage, bracing his weapon against a huge driftwood log in case the cats attacked. Xury and I loaded our guns.

The creatures left the people alone, plunging into the sea and splashing about as if for fun. When one came near our boat, I shot at its head: a good shot, for the animal sank beneath the surface. It bobbed up and tried to swim for shore, but never arrived. I watched it feebly sink into the shallow water, never to rise on its own.

Its companion fled at the sound of my shot, and the natives seemed inclined to do likewise, but when they saw the dead creature and no more threat to themselves, at my gestures they waded out to find the creature. The blood made this easy, and they hauled it ashore.

It was a very large leopard, and they seemed very impressed. They made signs that they would like to eat it, and I signaled that it was my gift to them. The women immediately set to work butchering out the big feline with great skill, far faster than I could have. I declined their offer of some of the meat, insisting that they have it all, but I made signs that I would like to have the hide. This they gave me freely, along with a lot more of their food. When I showed them an empty jar, two of the women led Xury to a fine water source from which he returned with three full jars. In this friendly atmosphere I bade the

Negroes thanks and farewell, and we got on our way once again.

With this increased food and water supply, we were able to proceed about eleven more days without landing. At that time I rounded a point extending very far out to sea, which I felt sure must be Cape Verde. I could see the islands in the distance. Should I try for them? My boat wasn't designed for the high seas, and if I was blown far offshore I might miss the islands and never get back.

I left Xury at the helm and went into the cabin to think. Then I heard him cry out, "Master, master, a ship with a sail!" He feared one of our old pirate master's ships come to get us, but that was ridiculous this far south of Sallee. I saw the flag of Portugal, but its course was counter to mine. In desperation, I brought our boat about and sailed toward them as fast as I could, but couldn't catch up. Just when I was beginning to despair, someone aboard must have spotted me, for the vessel shortened sail.

When I came alongside them, they queried me in Portuguese, Spanish, and French; I couldn't understand. At last a Scotsman called to me in English. I told him I was an English Christian, an escapee from Moorish slavery at Sallee, and Xury was a Moorish Muslim who had sworn service to me. They encouraged me to bring my goods and come on board.

What deliverance! In my joy, I offered all that I had to the captain, but he would take nothing. His ship was bound for Brazil, and there I would be able to disembark with all my possessions. Through the Scotsman he told me: "Perhaps someday I might be in your place; if so, I would want someone to save my life and treat me kindly. Besides, when we reach Brazil, you will be very far from your country. You will need what you have in order to survive. No, Senhor Inglese, I will carry you there at no charge."

The Portuguese captain kept his word. He ordered his men not to take anything of mine, on pain of punishment, then inventoried the lot and gave me the list. He liked my boat, and offered to buy it for his ship; what would I take for it? "I can't ask a price of you after you've been so generous to me," I said. "I leave that entirely up to you."

"Then," said he through his interpreter, "I will give you a note for eighty pieces of eight when we reach Brazil. If anyone offers you more, I will pay the difference." He also offered me sixty pieces of eight for Xury, but I hardly felt he was mine to sell after all his help toward my freedom. When I explained this, the captain said he understood, and made an offer: if Xury wished to take service with him, and converted to Christianity within ten years, he would be at liberty. Xury accepted, and that resolved all the business.

We had a very good three weeks' voyage to the Bay de Todos los Santos, as it is called. Now what? Thanks to the captain, my prospects were good. He would take no fare for my passage; he gave me sixty ducats for the leopard and lion skins, and had all my things delivered to me. He paid me fair prices for the rum, two of my guns, and the remainder of the beeswax. All told I went ashore in Brazil with around two hundred and twenty pieces of eight. As if that wasn't enough, the captain also recommended me to a local sugar planter, who he said was honest and helpful. I bade my benefactor and Xury a warm farewell.

The planter invited me to stay at his plantation, where I might learn how to raise sugar cane. He and the other planters were very wealthy, and I decided to begin my own plantation. In the meantime, I would see if I could have my money sent from London, and I bought as much uncleared land as I could afford. This would help me gain legal residence.

One of my neighbors was a man named Wells, a Portuguese born of English parents, struggling much as I was. We found camaraderie in our trials; at first we planted mainly for food. When we had enough clear land, we planted some tobacco, and prepared to plant sugar cane the next year. But now both of us needed help, and I began to wish I hadn't sent Xury off.

One day I was feeling particularly sore after a long day's work, and I took stock of myself. What had I achieved? I was living, but only by the sweat of my brow. For this I had forsaken my father's house and good advice—and only now was I coming into the "middle station of life." I could have managed that in England, among my friends, without going five thousand miles to toil among strangers in a wilderness. And strangers they were, for hardly anyone in Brazil knew me. Plantations were large and distances great; Wells was my main human contact. I felt like I'd been cast away on a deserted island. As I look back now, perhaps when I made this comparison, the Almighty heard it and decided I needed to see the difference. I can't know, but I do know that if I had stayed in Brazil, I would have become a wealthy, comfortable man.

I was very pleased when my kind friend, the Portuguese captain, stopped by a few months later to check on me. By this time I knew enough Portuguese to converse, and I told him about my money in London. "Senhor Inglese," he said, "if you will give me the proper letters, I will take them to Europe. I suggest you ask the lady to send your money to Lisbon in the form of trade goods that would sell well in this country, and I will bring them to you from there. But since nothing is certain, I suggest you give orders for only £100 at this time. If it comes safely, you can ask for the rest in the same way; if it doesn't, you will not have lost all."

This advice was wholesome. I sat down to write to the widow, giving her a full account of my endeavors, disasters, and adventures. I asked her to purchase English goods with half the money, and authorized her to consign them to the Portuguese captain.

This was all done better than I could have asked for. Not only did the widow fulfill her part, she gave the captain a present of £5 for his kindness to me. She engaged an English merchant to broker the goods and send them to Lisbon, from where they reached me safely in Brazil via my friend. The merchant had sensibly included all sorts of tools, utensils, and other ironwork necessary for a plantation. As for the captain, rather than accept the £5 for himself, he had used it to indenture a servant for me under terms of six years' bond. My friend would accept no reward for any of his services except a little of my tobacco, which I insisted he take.

My goods were of fine English manufacture: cloth, tools, and whatnot, and they fetched a fine sum in Brazil. When they were all sold I had four times their value, and was now far ahead of my poor neighbor. I even bought a Negro slave, and purchased the indenture of another European servant from a struggling planter who was giving up.

But abused success is often the cradle of

hardship, and so it was with me. In the next year, I raised fifty great rolls of tobacco, each weighing over a hundred pounds. I grew very impressed with myself, forgetting how much I owed to the kind generosity of others. By this time I'd been in Brazil four years, and had developed a good rapport with other planters and the merchants at our port of St. Salvador. I often told them of the Gold Coast, and how easy it was to make money there. One could trade minor goods for gold dust, grains, elephant tusks, and the like, or one could procure slaves for service in the Americas. The kings of Spain and Portugal controlled the slave trade, so that few Negro slaves were bought, and the price remained high.

The morning after an evening of this sort of discussion, three of my planter friends came to me with a proposal. After swearing me to secrecy, they explained that they had labor shortages similar to mine, and had a plan to alleviate this lack. They would fit out a ship bound for Africa, bring back Negro slaves, and rather than sell them publicly (which would get them thrown in jail for smuggling) the captives would simply be divided up and put to work. "What do you wish of me?" I asked.

"You seem to know that region," one said. "If you will go along, and manage the trading, you'll have your share of the slaves without having to invest any money."

"An attractive proposal, I must admit," I replied, "but who will manage my plantation while I'm gone?"

"We will sign an agreement to look after your lands as if they were our own. Before you go, you must make a will, so that if you are lost we know how to dispose of your assets."

It was all a great folly, of course. I was ready to send for my other £100 worth of goods from England, which would surely bring me another fine profit. I had but to stay on my plantation, and I would be comfortable in life. But I was born to be my own destroyer. I could no more resist this offer than I had been able to resist running off to sea in the first place. I agreed to their terms, and made out my will. I named the Portuguese captain as my beneficiary, with instructions to keep half my assets for himself and remit the other half to England—my one sensible act in the circumstances.

The ship was fitted out, the cargo furnished by agreement. On an evil hour, the 1st of September 1659, I went on board. On that same day eight years before, I had boarded the ship in Hull. Now St. Salvador was receding behind us. I was bound once more for Africa.

We had very good weather, albeit excessively hot, all the way to Cape St. Augustino. From there, we left sight of land and steered in the direction of the island Fernando de Noronha, which lies some two hundred miles from the easternmost reach of South America.

We passed these without incident, but at about 7° 22' North latitude, a violent hurricane came on us with very little warning. It shifted direction several times before settling in the northeast, whence it blew for twelve violent days. We could do little but batten down and hope. Everyone expected each day to be our last, and for three of us it was: one man died of a tropical fever, and a man and a boy were lost overboard.

On the twelfth day, when the storm let up a little, the captain took bearings. We had been blown far back up the northern coast of Brazil, off the coast of Guiana near the river Orinoco. He asked me what course he should take, for the ship was leaky and disabled, and he wanted to go back to the coast of Brazil. I opposed this, and we conferred over the charts of the South American coast. There were no nearby settlements, so we agreed to sail north for Barbados. That would probably take fifteen days or so, and there we could repair the ship and resume our voyage to Africa. If we failed to make Barbados, we might hope for assistance at any of the other Lesser Antilles.

In the end, we saw no Antilles of any kind. At about 12° 18' North, a second storm blasted us away westward, far from all European habitation. How far west, no man could say, but in the morning the wind was still quite strong when one man cried out: "Land!" As everyone was running out of the cabin to look, our ship struck a sandbar. The impact threw every man flat, and a tremendous wave sprayed over her. Unable to move with the sea, the water battered the vessel so badly we all took shelter in the cabin.

Only one who has experienced such a state can adequately describe it. We had no idea where we were, whether this was an island or the South American mainland, nor whether it was inhabited. Unless the wind miraculously died down, it would keep slamming the surf against our ship so hard it must soon break up. Each man prepared himself for the end.

After some time, the captain said that the wind seemed to be easing. We inspected and found much other news, none as good: the sea and wind had pounded us into the sand like some great nail. Getting away would be difficult, perhaps impossible. We had been towing a small boat astern; this had broken up against our rudder, then fallen away. Only one boat remained on board, but there was no guarantee we could lower it into the sea, much less of its seaworthiness.

There was no time to debate, for we could hear the crack of timbers with every vicious watery impact. The first mate ordered the boat lowered, and we remaining eleven climbed or leaped down into it, committing ourselves to the mercy of God and the sea. Though the storm had let up considerably, the sea yet ran dreadfully high on the shore—too high, we saw, for us to have much chance. We had no sail, nor any way to make it. We could only row for shore with heavy hearts, like men going to execution, and pray.

Our only hope now was some sort of sheltered bay, gulf, or river mouth, where we might escape the wind. We couldn't know if the sea bottom was rocky or sandy, steep or gradual. The nearer we came to shore, the more frightening the country appeared.

After we had rowed about four miles, a raging mountain of a wave came rolling astern of us. I believe every man knew that this was it. It took us with such a fury that we were all in the water before any man could cry out. Separated from boat and fellows, each man would have to deliver himself—if he could.

In my case, it was luck. I was a fine swimmer, but I couldn't get my head above that massive wave as it drove for shore. Desperate for air, I felt the water drag my body roughly across the sandy bottom, then stop as the breaker rolled onto the beach without me. While a wave was coming in, I was under water; while it was going out, as happened shortly, I could take in air.

I did more than breathe, for when I stood up

I saw another great monster of a wave bearing down. I made for dry land, but saw I would not make it and drew in a good deep breath to prepare for another bout of battering and submerging. I would have to try to swim for shore once I came up, hoping that the sea didn't drag me out as far as it had hurled me in. When the great wave washed over me, I was buried twenty or thirty feet deep in it, carried with mighty force toward the shore. I swam in that direction, a feeble gesture but at least an action, and held my breath as best I could.

With immense relief I felt my head and hands shoot above the surface of the water. I took a deep breath on the spot, and felt ground beneath my feet—but not for long. Twice again the sea picked me up and hurled me with its full power, the final time against a big rock. For a moment I was senseless, but I recovered prior to the next watery blow. This time I purposed to hang onto the rock for dear life and hold my breath. Since this spot was nearer land, the waves had spent more of their force, and my method worked. In between waves I would dash forward, take hold of a rock and brace myself. Before long I was able to clamber up the shore cliffs, sit down on the grass, and thank the Almighty.

A criminal on his way to hang when the notice of pardon arrives might feel much as I did. "For sudden joys, like grief, confound at first." I can vouch for the truth of the saying. I stood up and walked on shore to assess my situation. All my comrades looked to have drowned. I was the one soul saved; I never even found their bodies. Three of their hats did wash up, as did two unmatched shoes—nothing more.

I could see the stranded vessel, which seemed very far. How I had even got ashore was mysterious. Soon the euphoria of survival gave way to bitter reality. My clothes were in rags; all I had was a knife, a pipe, and a small box of tobacco. No food, nothing to drink, no shelter; if wild animals came, my knife would probably do me little good. For a while I ran about like a madman. In my ramblings I did find a bit of standing water, and quenched my thirst. I had no idea how to get food, so I put a bit of tobacco in my mouth to gain the illusion of food.

Around nightfall I realized I must find some form of safe rest, for many animals hunt at night. I found a thick, tall tree, a sort of fir but with thorns, and elected to spend the night there. Wedging myself so I wouldn't fall, I got as comfortable as I could. The immense fatigue of my fateful day soon overcame me, and I had a long, deep, refreshing sleep.

CHAPTER 4

First Months on the Island

I woke up in broad daylight. The weather had cleared; the sea was calm. I looked out to sea, and the ship was still intact—but had been dislodged and carried far closer to shore! I grew very sad, grieving both for my comrades and our bad judgment. Had we not abandoned ship in a panic, we might all still be alive. Perhaps we might have built a boat from the ruins, and made our way back to civilization.

Soon these melancholy thoughts gave way to wondering: what could I get from the ship? I came down from the tree and walked down to shore, and I saw our boat washed up some distance down the coast to my right. I would have to cross a large inlet to reach it, and decided this could wait. When the tide went far out, I could walk to within a quarter mile of the ship. I pulled off most of my clothes at water's edge, waded out, and began to swim.

I reached the ship's side easily enough, but I had not thought of how I would climb its tall sides and get aboard. I surely couldn't smash through the mighty timbers at the waterline. I swam around, wondering what to do, and on the second lap I spotted a small piece of rope hanging down near the fore chains. With great difficulty I got hold of it and climbed on deck. The ship was stuck deep into the sand, or mud, and angled so that the bow was lowest. I went down to the hold.

The hold had leaked badly. Anything stowed near the bow was likely to be spoiled; anything astern might be in good shape. Very fortunately, all the ship's food supplies were in the stern. I got a batch of ship's biscuit and a little rum, had lunch, and thought about how to get things ashore.

While I considered this, the ship's two cats (for rat control) and dog (as a pet) came up to me, begging. I shared the biscuit with them, and they began to keep me company. I would take them ashore, but they were the easiest part of that task. To get all the useful supplies on shore, I would need a raft. We had spare masts and lumber, a good amount of which I dragged topside. I raided the carpenter's work area for a saw and cut the masts into equal lengths. I was about to start throwing wood overboard and leap after it when I realized I would want a good way to get back up, so I tied a knotted rope to the mainmast for easier climbing. This done, I hove the wood over the side and climbed down after it, a coil of rope about my neck.

Once in the water I began to tie the boards and mast pieces together until I had a sturdy-looking raft. When I climbed onto it, I could see that it swamped and rocked easily, so I added reinforcement until it was more buoyant and stable. I moored it by the bow, where I would have the least distance to sway down my cargo, and climbed back up to start rummaging.

First I lowered down as much lumber as possible. I looked around and found three seamen's chests, which I emptied of their meager personal items. I needed the containers, and the first I filled with food: bread, rice, cheese, salted goat meat, and some European grain meant for the ship's chickens (which had not survived). There had also been barley and wheat, but rats had ruined or eaten it all. Next I found some bottles of rum and wine in the captain's cabin, and these went into the second chest.

While I filled that chest, I saw the tide starting in. Only then did I remember that I had foolishly left most of my clothes on the beach. I was helpless to stop them floating away, but after my moment of great disappointment, I realized that I should find some more clothes. Every seaman had some, and these made fine packing to keep the bottles from shattering. I put a few items into the third chest.

Half a chest was left to fill, and I realized it must be loaded with weapons if I were to have any safety ashore. I found two good bird guns in the great cabin, and two pistols and powder horns. Along with these, I took two bags of shot and bullets. I knew there were three barrels of powder aboard, and I found these at the edge of the waterline in the hold. One was soaked, but the other two were good and dry, well worth taking. Once all this was on deck, I began the work of lowering each item down to the raft, climbing down, releasing it and climbing back up to repeat the action.

I already knew what I wanted next: the carpenter's tool chest, more valuable to me than a shipload of gold. I found it in the same place I'd gotten the saw, and carried it topside without even inspecting the contents.

It was not far for the cats to leap down at my urging, and the dog I simply tossed overboard before my last descent. He could better cope with that than he could face being tied in a cradle of rope, which would badly frighten him. To my relief, the tide was still headed in, so I took a couple of broken oars and descended. The dog had already climbed onto my raft. He would throw off the balance, but I didn't want to make him swim all that way.

When depending on the tide for most of the work, I had limited ability to navigate. With help from my oars, the sea carried me in toward the wide inlet I had seen earlier that day. I cooperated with the tide until I saw a small stream emptying into the inlet, and guided my craft toward this river mouth.

As I soon learned, navigation is hazardous when you don't know the changes in depth. Near the river mouth my raft ran around on a shoal and tipped upward. My goods began sliding off the raft, and I scrambled to the low side to hold them back with my body. To lose them, I believe, would have broken my heart. The cats and dog were no help, running around nervously. I had to brace myself that way for nearly half an hour until the tide lifted us level again, and I paddled into the river mouth in search of a likely landing spot.

It wouldn't do to go too far upstream, if that were even possible, because I wanted to keep an eye out to sea for ships. At length I spied a little cove on the right shore of the creek, with a tree close by to moor my raft, and climbed ashore to rest awhile.

When I felt refreshed, I felt an urge to explore. Where would I make my home? Secure my goods? I didn't even know whether this was an island, the South American mainland, or wherever. Were there humans? Predatory animals? I could see a hill perhaps a mile from me,

so I took a bird gun and a pistol and climbed toward the highest point to survey my new world.

I was on a small, forested island with some valleys and hills, with no other land in sight but some distant rocks and two smaller islands a few miles west. I saw no sign of wild animals, but many birds. Were any of them fit for food? There was only one way to find out, and on the way back, I shot a great bird sitting on the edge of a forest. Thousands of other birds rose screaming at the noise, none of which sounded or looked familiar. My kill was a kind of hawk, unfortunately—not good to eat.

Back I went to my landing cove. It was time I consider my nighttime safety, for any number of hungry beasts might prowl this land. All I had was my load of goods, and these I arranged in a sort of circle around me. It was the world's smallest fortress, but it was what I had. I braced up chests and barrels with the lumber. Hopefully the cats and dog would keep good enough watch during the night. They might also hunt, for I had seen some rabbitlike creatures run out of the forest when I shot the hawk.

After a safe and relatively comfortable night, in the morning I called a council of my thoughts. For every useful thing I'd gotten from the ship, which might break up at any moment, a dozen more remained aboard. It was the rainy season, and surely the next storm would finish the ship for good. Home-building would have to wait until I got every board, barrel, box, bottle, sail, rope, gun, tool, or whatever else that I could get ashore. The practical method was to go out with the ebbing tide, load up, then return with the inbound tide. Without a moment to lose, I brought along some biscuit for breakfast and began to guide my raft out to the treasure-trove.

With more experience and a raft already built, this trip was more efficient. I got some bags of nails and spikes, a screw jack, more than a dozen hatchets and a grindstone from the carpenter's stores. The gunner's storage held three iron crowbars, two barrels of musket bullets, a large bag of shot, seven muskets, another bird gun, and some more powder. A great roll of sheet lead was too heavy to hoist up. I then raided the crew's quarters and sailmaker's work area for clothes, spare sails, a hammock, and some bedding. Down the rope I went, and caught the inbound tide for my cove.

Just as I had plundered the ship's goods, and would plunder more, I worried that something might do the same to mine ashore while I was away. Fortunately, when I came back I saw no sign of any visitor, not even the cats and dog which were apparently off doing whatever their kind do when abandoned on remote islands. I got busy making myself a little tent, for my own shelter and to keep the sun and rain off my goods. When this was all finished I had a rude hut, greatly inferior to anything a native could have built but serving my purpose. I spread out my bedding and slept with weapons nearby.

The third day's voyage got me most of the rigging, every rope and spool of twine I could find, a spare sail canvas, and the barrel of wet gunpowder. The next few voyages brought ashore the remainder of the ship's portable goods. These included a barrel of bread—a wonderful find! In this same place I also found three kegs of rum, a barrel of flour and a box of sugar. I then began salvaging the immense anchor cable, several inches thick, which had to be cut into lengths. For a few days I hacked, sawed, and cut away parts of the ship I thought I might use.

It rained intermittently, but I couldn't afford to slow down. I spent much of the time soaked to the skin.

Then I had a very bad day. My journal reminds me that it was October 20—my twentieth day ashore. By that time I was down to the actual masts and all the ironwork I could hoist down to the raft, but this proved too unwieldy a load. Just as I entered the cove, the misbalanced raft tipped up and dumped goods—and Crusoe—over the side. I lost all the ironmongery, but recovered all the mast pieces. In later days, at low tide, I would recover some of the iron.

After twenty-three days I had made eleven trips. Had the weather cooperated, I might have brought the whole ship ashore piece by piece. But as I embarked on my twelfth, the wind began to rise. I had begun to have a sense of the local weather, and I focused this trip on any loose or hidden goods I had previously overlooked. In this process I found a locker concealed behind some of the captain's furniture. It contained three razors, a pair of large scissors, a dozen table-knives and forks, and about thirty-six pounds in European, Brazilian, and other gold and silver coin.

I smiled to myself at the sight of this money: "You drug!" said I. "Greed for you brought me here, and now you're worthless to me. One of these knives is worth every coin. Go down with the ship, and be cursed." Then I had second thoughts, and decided to take it along. On deck I saw the sky growing overcast, with the wind working up to a gale, so I made haste down to my raft. I got back to my cove just as the gale turned to a full-blown storm.

I slept through most of the storm, secure in my little tent. When I awoke in the morning, my twenty-fifth day, the wind had moderated but it was still raining. As I hurried to put extra cover over my goods, I looked out to sea and saw that the ship had broken completely apart. Some loose parts were already washing ashore, and the remainder would wither until it was only visible at low tide. What a relief it was that I had worked hard while I had the chance, and got everything useful I could bring away.

Now, as my journal tells me, I resolved to find a permanent home. I needed shelter from the weather and predators, dry storage for my goods, and a nearby source of fresh water. My current location, with its salty water and swampy, unhealthy air, was not suitable. If I caught a tropical fever, I would probably die in misery. As I headed off to explore, I considered whether I ought to build a tent, a cave, or a hut. Besides shelter and water, I wanted a view out to sea. I hiked toward higher ground and kept a careful eye out for good options.

After wandering most of the day, I came to a promising spot. I was on a hill of mostly gentle slope, except where a steep rocky wall fronted a meadow perhaps the size of a sporting field. The steep part had a slight hollow, as though nature had begun a cave then canceled the project, and the rock looked movable and breakable. This faced nearly northward, giving it shade most of the day. From the plateau, the land sloped gently down to the seaside. A small spring bubbled out of the earth some short way down this slope. This was definitely the place.

I marked out a semicircle against the stony hillside, about ten yards out and twenty wide, and managed to carry up some of the thick cable lengths and mast pieces before nightfall. The next day I got to work in full earnest.

My idea was to build a walled tent, sort of a semi-hut, entered by climbing over. All doorways are the weakest part of any wall. For this to work well, I must first get all my things inside, so I began carrying my goods up the hill. Load by load the pile inside my enclosure increased, and I made it into the same sort of temporary tent fort it had formed by the cove. This would keep me and my things sheltered until the main structure was finished. When the cats and dog came around, I fed them; otherwise I let them care for themselves.

I began by cutting small trees and mast pieces

to lengths of nearly seven feet. I drove each into the ground along the semicircular line I had marked, with perhaps a foot between them. The work was exhausting, for at first I pounded the stakes with a large piece of wood; it got easier when I remembered I could use one of the heavy crowbars. Six inches inside the first half-circle, I drove a second semicircle of stakes, then sharpened all the tops. Between the two rows, I laid lengths of anchor cable on top of each other until I had a thick wall enclosing my space. It was about five and a half feet high, just about my own height.

For an entrance, I built two short ladders, one for each side of the wall. Over my enclosure I pitched the ship's huge mainsail, sloping from eight feet high against the hillside down to the wall. It rained the entire time, which taught me that I must make it very tight and consider where the water would run off. I decided to cut a single long pole for the middle, to be the high part, so that the rain would pour off the sides rather than pool up and leak through. Happily, all ships carry a great amount and variety of rope. I had more than enough to secure my roof.

After I had been at this work for five days, I started going on hunting trips to break up the dullness. I saw a herd of goats, and found that they kept a good watch except when I got above them, and soon I shot one. When I went down into the valley to get my kill, I saw that it was a nanny, whose poor orphan stood there frightened and bewildered. I took the little creature home, but he wouldn't eat, and I ended up eating him. I preserved the skins, and did the same with a wildcat I got a few days later; the only use for the meat was to feed the dog. As my hunting partner, he had earned a good meal.

My journal tells me I was now into early November, and I began to keep a schedule. Every morning I went out hunting for two or three hours, unless it rained. When I returned, I would work on my structure until lunchtime at eleven. Between noon and two was the hottest part of the day, so I napped through it, returning to my work in the afternoon. My hut improved each day. As soon as I secured my roof, I strung my hammock outside the temporary shelter, leaving that in place just in case. I began making a table and chair, with many imperfections due to my lack of carpentry expertise.

One day as I ate, I realized that I was in danger of losing track of time. I cut a large post, joined another piece to it to form a cross, and set it up on shore where I had first washed up. On it I carved: "I came on shore here the 30th of September, 1659." Into the sides of this square post, I cut a notch each day with my knife. Every seventh cut was twice as wide as the rest, and that for the first of every month wider still. On each trip down, I picked up whatever ship pieces looked most useful.

Here I should mention that I wanted the table and chair for more than just a place to sit and eat. In addition to the primary items I had saved from the ship, there was a large assortment of secondary goods: pens, ink, paper, some parcels entrusted to the captain, compasses, mathematical instruments, navigational charts and books, three Bibles in English, some Portuguese prayer books, and a small assortment of other reading matter. I conserved ink and paper to the utmost, for I could not replenish them. While I wished for much else—more ink, a shovel, a wheelbarrow, a pick, needles, thread, pins, and bolts of cloth—I had reason to be glad of what I had. Perhaps I could manufacture what I needed.

The work was tedious, especially for lack of tools, but what else had I to do besides hunt? I learned to make do with what I had. When I was pleased with my outer wall and roof, I began carving my way into the hillside with crowbars. The resulting dirt and rocks I carried to my wall, laying them down at first as a terrace. Eventually I would raise this into an earthen wall, to further strengthen my fortress.

Against some dangers, of course, few fortresses were much good. One stormy day I got an early start on my cave digging. There came a terrific flash, then a great "boom!" quite close by. That meant a very near lightning strike, and I looked toward the woods to see a newly shattered tree. What if that bolt had struck my hut and into my powder kegs? I would at least have felt no pain, for I would have been blown to fragments. I set aside my tools and got to work dividing up all my powder into smaller containers, which was much work as I had over two hundred pounds of the stuff. I cached each powder container under earth and rocks in the hillside, well apart from others, so that a single bolt from Heaven could not so easily erase Robinson Crusoe from existence. The wet barrel didn't worry me as much, but as my cave took shape it was the first thing to go inside.

As November drew on, I made good progress into the hillside. During one morning's hunt, I found a tree I knew from Brazil: the iron-wood. This tree is made of such strong stuff it can ruin any axe, and indeed it nearly ruined mine. With great labor I cut off a large, low branch and lugged it home. To my daily work I added the job of carving this into a shovel, and soon I finished—though never, I believe, did anyone work so hard to make a shovel.

As for a wheelbarrow, I lacked some very important parts, but I could fashion a substitute. I thought of bricklayers, and how they carried their heavy loads in a contrivance known as a "hod." I might do the same, so I took lumber and nails and assembled a small sort of semi-box.

It looked as though I had cut a chest lengthwise into diagonal halves. I bored holes on the sides for a rope to sling behind my neck, and along the diagonal cuts I cut wider holes for handholds. I could easily push earth and rocks into this, slip the rope over my neck, steady it with my hands, stand up, and carry it wherever I wished.

Around early December, my cave grew wide enough to consider relocating my goods inside. The heavier rains gave incentive, and I had to take time to reinforce my dwelling's roof. Eventually I wanted my cave to serve as warehouse, kitchen, dining room, and cellar. Just as I began to think it was coming along quite well, part of the ceiling caved in. Had I been standing in that place, it would surely have become my tomb. Once I carried out the loose earth and rock, I began to shore up the roof using poles and lumber. Some of the shoring along the side also supported shelves which I built; nails driven into the poles served to hang things up. While the shelf-making nearly used up my ready supply of boards, it enabled me to carry all my goods into the cave.

All this time I had started keeping a daily journal, without which I would have forgotten much of this story many years ago. This document tells much about my thoughts on life, for I had all the time to think one man could ever wish. My outlook was quite dismal. It appeared to me that God had condemned me to end my days in lonely exile. Many times I wept, and often raged and pleaded: "Why would the Almighty make one of his creatures so miserable?" Lacking a debating partner, I debated myself: "Yes, your condition is bad, but not so bad as your shipmates'. The other ten are dead. Why were you saved, and not they? Who is worse off?" Thus I learned that all bad fortune must be considered along with whatever good it brings, and how much worse it could be.

When I stopped to think about it, I had my share of good fortune. What if the ship had not been floated nearer to shore, for example? How would I have gotten so many useful things, such as weapons, and tools, and bedding, and clothing? I might well be naked, sleeping in the wet, starving, hunting desperately with such spears as I might be able to make. My death would have been slow and horrid. If I planned sensibly, I might be well provided against the day my ammunition would run out, even against the time when my health and strength faded with age.

One day I made a list of the good and evil facts of my condition, which helped me very much to learn to look at the positive. I set them down like a merchant listing his assets and debts:

Evil: I am cast upon a horrible, desolate island, with no hope of rescue.

Good: But I am not drowned, as everyone

else was, nor am I starving.

Evil: I am all by myself, singled out from society.

Good: He who spared my life may yet spare me from loneliness somehow.

Evil: I have few clothes, and these are fast wearing out.

Good: I am in a hot climate, often too hot for many clothes anyway.

Evil: I am nearly defenseless.

Good: There seems to be nothing here to threaten me. What if I had been shipwrecked on the coast of Africa, where the fiercest beasts in all the world hunt each other and mankind?

Evil: I have no one to talk to but myself. (As you can see, this was perhaps my greatest lasting source of melancholy.)

Good: I have books, and materials for this journal, and a dog and cats.

Evil: I have immense labor just to build a living space and find food.

Good: But God wonderfully sent the ship in where I could get supplies, which in turn will enable me to supply myself.

This was a turning point for me. I had developed the sorrowful habit of looking forlornly out to sea, in desperate hope of spotting a sail. Now I quit this bad practice, which only harmed my mood, and directed my energies toward what I could change. With the debris from cave carving,

I raised the terrace along my wall until it reached the tops of the poles, and I added rafters to strengthen my roof. I turned right in my caving, then right again, so that I exited the hillside at a point outside my wall. Now I had a back entrance, a way in and out without using the ladder, as well as much more storage space.

Here is an example of why the work took so long. In civilization, if one wants a board, one buys it from a sawyer. I had to cut down a tree and saw or chop my own boards, which took a great deal of time and effort. Using these, plus such scrap lumber as washed ashore from the wreck, I extended my shelves all along the left side of my cave. I perfected my table and chair, which gave me a comfortable place to eat, keep my journal, and read. It was perhaps good that I had lacked the means to keep this journal at first, for I can imagine what I might have written: "30th—After I got to shore, and escaped drowning, instead of thanking God for my safety, I first vomited up all the salt water I had swallowed. Then I ran about the shore wringing my hands and weeping, crying out, 'I am ruined! Ruined!' until I lay down in exhaustion, but didn't dare sleep for fear of being eaten."

As the new year of 1660 approached, I tried to look ahead rather than backward. I had much to do and learn.

CHAPTER 5

The Earth Shakes, and with It My Spirit

*A*s I neared New Year's Day, my loose-knit animal community expanded. On a hunting trip I shot two young goats, killing one and breaking the other's leg. I led the injured animal home, splinted the injury and set the little creature in my meadow to graze. After he healed, he preferred to stay, which gave me an idea: if I could raise a herd of them, I would have food after my powder and shot ran out.

Some days were very hot, others were very rainy, and plenty were hot and rainy. I added a turfed earthen wall outside my cable-and-post wall's perimeter. If any people came ashore, they might not even spot my home. One day, in fact, this came in very handy—but all in its proper time.

I also hunted as the weather permitted, and on these walks I often made discoveries or got ideas. I found a breed of wild pigeons that nested in holes in the rocks, and took some young ones back to my hillside in hopes of taming them, but I found them difficult to feed and ended up having them for dinner. I would look for evidence of animals, useful plants, new types of trees—anything that might change my existence, or help me remedy my many and glaring wants. I had no barrels, for example, nor the ability or tools to make them. No candles; the best I could do there was to collect the tallow from slain goats, and use it in a sort of oil lamp. One stroke of good fortune came, oddly enough and a bit indirectly, from rats.

At one point the previous fall, I had been sifting through my goods and found some grain originally meant for the chickens. What little remained was fouled and chewed by rats, and I needed the bag for something else, so I shook out the remnants and thought nothing more of it. I happened past that spot a couple of months later and got a wonderful surprise: a patch of perfect green English barley had sprouted. What was more, near this patch were stalks of rice, as I had seen on my travels in Africa.

The sight of this little cluster of growing grain, with all that it meant for my food supply, deeply affected my soul. At first I didn't make the connection between my discarded grain and this new growth, and it seemed that God had favored me with a miracle. I began looking all over the place for more such grain, but found none, and finally realized how the plants had come about.

Whatever the reason, the grain had fallen someplace fertile, and enough had been unspoiled to grow. I watched it carefully, and made plans to save the rice and barley for replanting. Months passed, and in April, I had just begun to feel my dwelling was nearly finished. Then a terrible disaster almost destroyed all my work—and me with it.

I was working at the cave entrance, making some minor improvement or other, when the earth began to shake. The cave roof began to fall in, except where I had bolstered it with supports, and two of my posts made frightful cracking sounds. I ran forward and climbed out by the ladder, then got away from the steep hillside in case of avalanche. I huddled down against the trembling earth, through which I felt several mighty tremors in the space of half an hour. At one point a great rock came crashing down the hill, fortunately nowhere near me, and plunged into the ocean with a mighty splash. From the turmoil and roil of the sea, I suspect the shocks were stronger under the water than on my island.

Never in my life had I experienced such a thing, nor spoken with anyone who had. It made my stomach sick, somewhat like my first voyage. I feared that the hillside would bury all my things, and with them all my hard work hopes of comfort. My heart sank to great depths.

After the third shock was over, and I felt no more for some time, I began to compose myself. I didn't go back inside for fear of being buried alive. I sat still on the ground, terribly sad, with no idea what to do. I had no religious thoughts beyond the expected reflex "Lord, have mercy upon me!" When the tremors ended, so did that sentiment.

While I was worrying and thinking, the sky clouded over. The wind soon came up, little by little, growing into a full-blown hurricane. The sea was all foam and froth, and the storm tore trees up by the roots. My tent might be blown down around me, so I went back into my cave and hoped there would be no more earth tremors. Whether the quake somehow caused the storm—if such a thing is even possible—I do not know. I do recall that it blew for three hours before it faded to a simple if dreary rain.

In the drizzling aftermath of the tremors, I wondered: should I move my tent? I could withstand April storms, but if earthquakes were frequent, the whole hillside might bury me at any time. I spent the next two days in search of a better spot, goaded on by my nightly fear of entombment. The more I searched, the more I preferred my existing home; also, the more I realized how much work it would be to relocate. I decided to build a fully circular wall of posts and cable somewhere in the open, then set my tent up inside, but not to move there until the new place was complete. I could take my time.

Tools began to be an issue. I had three large axes and many more hatchets (originally intended for trade), but these had grown all notched and dull chopping hard, knotty wood. I had a grindstone, but it took two people to operate. I spent as much thought on this as a judge might on a man's life or death. Finally I thought of a way I could rig a string and wheel, to turn the stone with my foot. I had never seen this in England, but I have now learned how common it is there.

After a week of experimenting and erring, my grindstone mechanism worked well. Sharpening all my tools occupied another pair of days, and then it was nearly May. My bread began to run low, and I had to cut my ration to one biscuit a day.

On the morning of May 1, I was lazing about looking out to sea at low tide. Something had washed ashore, larger than the usual wreckage and such, and I went down to see. In addition to some more ship pieces, a small barrel had washed up on shore intact. It was...gunpowder! But it was soaked, of course, and was packed hard as stone. Even so, I rolled it above the tide line for later consideration.

From this vantage, I noticed that the wreck had shifted higher in the water and nearer the shore. I could now wade out to it at low tide.

When I reached the forlorn remnant of the doomed vessel, it was more broken up than before, and the hold had filled up with sand. While I would get nothing useful from this sandy burial, I might pull, hack or saw off any number of useful parts above it. I postponed my plans for a new dwelling, and got to work salvaging what I could. As I worked, I watched the shore more closely than usual for helpful items that might wash ashore.

To break up the monotony of these early May and June days of sawing, prying, and whatnot, I went fishing. I dried my catches in the sun and ate those I felt were safe. On days when the tide was unfavorable, I went hunting instead. One June morning I found a large turtle, the first I had seen, making me think they were very scarce here. (I later learned that was an accident of my location. Had I washed up on the other side of the island, I could have had hundreds per day, though I might have paid dearly for them, as I also learned in time.) This turtle was a female, about to lay eggs, and she was the tastiest meal I could recall since landing in this horrid place.

The punishing heat made my work exhausting, but I had to keep going. Meanwhile, the combination of my salvage work and the pressure of the elements was tearing the wreck apart. Again I found the roll of sheet lead, but it was simply too heavy, plus partly buried and submerged. I mostly got ironwork and lumber, with a few barrels here and there. Some things came loose and floated ashore, such as two seamen's chests and a large barrel of spoiled pork. With great effort and in several pieces, I managed to cut away perhaps a hundred pounds of the sheet lead.

On June 18, I stayed in my hut to avoid a daylong and abnormally chilly rain. As my chill grew worse I realized I was becoming ill. There were terrible headaches and fever; I prayed sometimes, but couldn't write, and later I could hardly remember much of what I'd said. I remember it in delirious, disjointed bursts of misery.

My sickness came and went for nine days, alternating chills, feverish fits, and times of relative comfort. When I could, I hunted, for I was very hungry and the short rations were not helping my health.

During the 27th I was so violently ill I lay in bed all day, too weak even to get water. In my light-headed state, I prayed again: "Lord, please take pity on me! Please have mercy!" I fell asleep, and woke refreshed but weak and very thirsty. I drifted back to sleep, and then I had the most terrible dream.

My nightmare began with me sitting on the ground, outside my wall. A man bright as flame, even as blinding as sunlight, descended from a great black cloud to land before me. His face, to the extent I could gaze upon it, was indescribably dreadful—not ugly, but intimidating. In his hand he carried a long spear, and his every step shook the earth. When he came near me, he spoke in a terrifying voice: "Seeing that all thy calamities have not caused thou to repent, now thou shalt die." He raised his spear as if to impale me.

I awoke in the greatest terror of my life. This fear did not wear off much, and it got me thinking of how I had lived. I had never been very religious. My father had taught me something of faith, but eight years of seafaring wickedness and constant contact with others as profane as myself had pushed that faith aside. I had thought little about my soul except when in danger, at which time I pleaded for salvation and forgot gratitude as soon as I was safe. I had considered only worldly things: wealth, comfort, safety.

Now I saw myself as a sort of brute. To satisfy my whims, I had rebelled against my father. The Portuguese captain had rescued and aided me, and I had been grateful to him, but not to God for bringing him. When I was shipwrecked, I simply assumed that I was meant to be miserable, without considering why I alone might have been spared. The sprouting of the grain and rice influenced me a little, but not for long. Even the earthquake made no lasting spiritual impression. Nothing dented the armor of my self-centered outlook.

In short, I had come to resemble most of the sailors I had known, who would readily pray for safety from a storm and then, once they got that safety, would show their appreciation by getting drunk. I began to feel deeply sorry for the life of waste and greed I had led, and in my depression I prayed much as I had before: "Lord, I am miserable! I may die of this sickness! What will become of me?" Then I went on a binge of weeping.

As my tears flowed, I recalled my father's advice: if I took the foolish course I intended, God would not bless me, and when I truly needed help there would be no one to give it. I spoke aloud: "He was right. I could have lived a happy, easy life; instead, I left my parents to mourn my foolishness, and now I in turn am left to mourn its result. Divine Justice has struck me down." In my despair, I uttered my first real, sincere prayer in many years: "Lord, help me, for I am in great distress." What might come of it, I could not know.

I did know that I was terribly hungry and thirsty, so I drank my fill from the spring and filled a large water bottle in anticipation of the next bout of fever. I roasted some goat meat and had it with three turtle eggs I had saved, and I had the impulse to ask a blessing before I ate—perhaps the first time I had ever sincerely done so in my life. I was still sick and weak, but I reflected over my meager meal. If God had tossed me ashore here, and had in fact made all things, then He knew I was here. He knew my condition. He alone could save or condemn me. I asked: "Lord, why did you do this to me?"

The response came in my fevered mind as a thunderous reply to blasphemy: "Wretch! Dost thou ask what thou hast done? Look back on thy misspent life. Ask thyself—what hast thou *not* done? Why wert thou not drowned in Yarmouth Roads, or killed in the fight with the pirates, or eaten by wild beasts in Africa, or drowned here, as were all of thy shipmates? And thou dare ask what *I* have done?"

My first thought was to take some tobacco for my illness, as they do in Brazil, but then I realized I had a wiser remedy close to hand. Among the books from the wreck I had Bibles, and now I took one out and began to read at a random page. The words seemed to reach out to me from the paper: "Call on Me in the day of trouble, and I will deliver thee, and thou shalt glorify Me."

How apt those words were! Though at the time I had no idea how I might be delivered, this verse was engraved on my brain, and for many years I thought of it often. It was now late, and I went to bed. But before I did so, I did something I had never before done: I knelt by my bed, and prayed to God to fulfill the promise in the Scriptures.

I slept an exceedingly long time, all the next day and night (or so I later came to believe, when I saw the tides happen at the wrong times, for I had come to know these perfectly), and woke up around three in the afternoon of the 29th. I was stronger, livelier, and full of healthy hunger. The next day I felt up to a bit of hunting, and within a couple more days my illness was nearly gone. As my strength returned, my mind kept returning to the Bible verse. Had I not been delivered from sickness and misery? Should I not show gratitude? I knelt to pray my thanks aloud.

It was July 4 when I began the habit of reading a bit of the New Testament each morning and night. The more I read, the more my past bothered me, and the more comfort I took in my growing faith. I ceased to pray for rescue from the island, for I saw my loneliness as proper punishment for my reckless life. Instead I sought deliverance from the guilt of my multiple sins, and guidance as to how I might do better.

Thus I thought as I went through the slow process of recovery. My physical wellness might once again be the same, but my spiritual outlook never would.

CHAPTER 6

Farming

I had been on this unhappy island over ten lonely months with faint hope of rescue. But while there were no friendly people, there were also no unfriendly; there simply were none at all. Perhaps I was the first human being to walk here. With my home secure, I grew curious about this island of mine. What might I find?

My journal advises that I began this process on July 15. I first worked my way up the creek where I had landed my raft-loads of goods. This ran for perhaps two miles before declining to a little brook, fresh and good but with hardly any water in this, the dry season. Along the brook I found wild tobacco, sugar cane, aloes, and many unfamiliar plants. What I wanted most was cassava, for the Indians of that region make bread from it, but there was none. As I walked, I thought of how I might learn uses for some of the plants. What Indians knew from childhood, I must now learn by trial and error.

The next day I went back the same way, somewhat further, until the brook petered out in a forest. I found some melons along the ground, and grape vines absolutely covering the trees. The grapes were just now in their ripe, rich prime, but I remembered stories of men who had died from eating too many. I would dry them into raisins, which I could enjoy when there were no fresh grapes to be had at all. I spent the night away from home, the first time since the ship-wreck, sleeping in a tree just as I had done then.

In the morning I continued up the gentle valley. When I had gone about four miles, the country began to descend westward into lush, green lands watered by a little spring. All was in constant flower and flourish. I surveyed this delicious country with a certain pride of owner-ship, for I was lord of this manor, with none to challenge my whim or my rights. This lovely country was like a pantry of delicious things. I found an abundance of cocoa trees, as well as orange, lime, and lemon trees. I tasted some limes and found them delightful, but even better when their juice was squeezed into water.

I could have spent days there, but it was high time I prepared for the upcoming rainy season. I gathered up two great heaps of grapes, then one large pile of limes and lemons. I took a few of each with me, and resolved to hurry back with bags for the remainder. Had I any sense, I would have brought a bag to begin with. When I got home, the grapes were spoiled and broken; only the lemons and limes were still in good condition.

The next day, the 19th, I went back to my lovely vale with two bags. When I reached my heap of grapes, imagine my surprise to find half of them devoured and the other half tromped on! Obviously some sort of wild creatures were about. Because I couldn't lay grapes in heaps or carry a great quantity home, I took another course. I gathered up more grapes and hung the bunches up in trees to dry into raisins, then car-ried back as many limes and lemons as my bags would hold.

Once back home, I couldn't stop thinking of that fruitful valley. It was beautiful, rich in food, sheltered from storms. I began to think I had chosen the worst possible spot on the island to make my home, and I thought I might relocate. Then I remembered that a view of the sea had its own advantages, such as the ability to spot passing ships. If I moved deep inland, I would forsake all chance of rescue or companionship. I compromised: I would build a residence in the vale, a strong double fence studded with brushwood, entered only by a ladder and covered with a tent.

I got started immediately, making rapid progress due to past experience. By August 3rd, I had finished my country home and could relax. I had hung up about two hundred bunches of grapes, which had dried to perfectly good raisins. In mid-August, as I was gathering these up for storage, it started to rain. A good thing I got them into the cave in time, for the rain persisted until mid-October, sometimes confining me to shelter for days at a time.

In this season I was surprised to see my family increase. For days I had worried about one of my cats, who had been absent an abnormally long time. Just when I began to think she had died, to my astonishment she came home with three kittens. I didn't know how that was possible. I had seen a few very shy wildcats on the island, but these had been a different and much larger breed than our European house cats, and both of my cats were female. In any case, the cats multiplied until they became almost a plague that I had to kill or drive off, if I didn't want them always trying to break into my stored food. At least I had no rats.

During this bout of downpour, I made sure not to get too wet. This meant that food ran low, but I ventured out on two hunts, getting a goat and a large tortoise. How unfortunate that I didn't have a practical way to boil or stew anything—but at least I had raisins and meat. This was a good time to expand my cave, widening it and turning right until I exited the hillside outside my wall. Now I could get in and out without climbing the wall, though I had also lessened my security. At some point, I would have to remedy that—even though the largest creature I'd seen on the island was a goat.

One late September day I counted the notches on my post, and indeed, this was the thirtieth: the anniversary of my landing. I decided that this should be a day of solemn fasting and prayer, confessing and asking forgiveness for my sins. I didn't eat until nightfall, and while I had my biscuit and raisins, I reflected that I had been ignoring the Sabbath. Unfortunately, I had no idea which day was Sunday, for I had neglected to make the week marks for some time. I also suspected I might have missed a day somewhere. With no way to be certain, I designated this day as Sunday, and resolved not to forget it in the future.

Right about this time my ink began to run low. To conserve it, I would have to confine my journaling to the most important events. Now that I had a good sense of the island's seasons, I decided it was time to plant the barley and rice I'd saved. I spaded up a piece of ground and planted my grain, holding back a third of my seed just in case I was wrong.

A good thing I did, because I had blundered. Not a single grain sprouted in season, for the earth got no moisture at all during the dry months. I assumed that this was due to a drought and dug up another piece of ground near my inland residence, planting the rest of the seed in February. The March and April rains made this crop flourish, and some of the first seed also sprouted—though not as much as I'd have gotten had I planted it at the right time. My first crop wasn't very large, about enough of each to fill two water pails (had I owned any), but it was a start.

The most important farming concern was to adjust my mind to a new climate. In Europe we divide the year into summer and winter, but here it was different—and more promising. From mid-February to mid-April, it rained heavily. It was then dry until mid-August, when the rain returned for two months. From mid-October to mid-Feburary, all dry. If I farmed well, I might get two crops of rice and barley per year.

In about November, when the rains were completely over, I went to check on my country home. I found nearly everything as I'd left it, except for one area that had actually improved. My double row of stakes had taken root and sprouted long branches. Whatever type of tree I had cut to make them—I suspect it was some sort of willow—it was a treasure. I decided to plant a semicircle of them in front of my seaside dwelling, to give it cover and perhaps serve as a defense.

Now that I knew the seasons, I settled into a pattern: lay up provisions in the dry season, stay inside when it poured. In confinement, I experimented with many crafts, some more successful than others. I tried every way I could think of to make a basket, but none of the twigs I got proved elastic enough. Luckily, as a lad I had often stood at the basket-maker's and offered to help, in the eager and enthusiastic way of children. I knew the whole method; I simply lacked materials. Then I remembered the willowy trees I had cut for stakes, how soft and pliable their wood was. This material met my need. While my baskets were not especially attractive, they were functional—and who was nearby to criticize them anyhow?

Baskets were fine for solid storage and carrying, but liquids were another matter. I had a couple of small barrels of rum, but while this lasted, these were unavailable. Most of the barrels I had salvaged were leaky. I had some glass bottles, and a great kettle I had saved from the ship—perfect for cooking for an entire ship's company, but inconveniently large for my purposes. I didn't find a solution to the liquid problem, but between planting my new stakes and basket weaving, I kept well occupied until the dry season. Then another business came along that took up far more time than I could have imagined.

CHAPTER 7

Surveys His Position

I mentioned before that I hoped to explore the whole island. I suspected it wasn't far to the shore from my country home, so one day I decided to see. I took my gun, a hatchet, the dog, a good supply of powder and shot, and some biscuits and raisins to sustain me.

Not far past my pleasant vale, I saw the sea to the west. The day was quite clear, and I thought I saw mountains in the distance. Whether it was an island or the South American continent I had no idea; I guessed it was over thirty miles away. Most likely it was part of the vast New World Spanish dominions, perhaps the home of natives with bitter experience of Europeans. Maybe my marooning here had been divine mercy, keeping me safe from potential hostiles. This marked a change for me, quieting my mind so that I ceased to wish myself off my island.

By the same token, if I was seeing land

claimed by the King of Spain, surely Spanish ships might pass one way or another. It might also be the unsettled land between Brazil and Venezuela, home of the fiercest natives in South America. I had even heard tales of cannibalism. I reminded myself to keep alert as I walked down to the sea.

This side was indeed much pleasanter than the other. It was a land of sweet fields with flowers and deep grass, fine forests, and an abundance of parrots. I thought it would be very nice to catch and tame a parrot, and teach it to speak, but they were skittish and it took me some time to capture a young one. In the end it took him years to learn to call me by name.

The country here was all I could wish for. I found rabbits and foxes, goats and pigeons, and above all turtles. On my side I had found only three turtles in over a year; this shore was covered with them. Despite the pleasure of the trip and the promising food situation, I had no urge to move here. I was too comfortable with my existing home.

I kept going along the seashore to the east—I suppose about twelve miles. When I thought I was at the easternmost reach, I set up a pole on the shore as a mark. I decided I would go home, then journey to the far side of the island, until I came to my post again. This would give me a better idea of the size of my lands. I took a different way back, thinking that I would be able to see far enough to find my way home easily, but I was mistaken in this. I wound up in a deep valley where my only navigational guide was the sun—and then only if I knew its proper position at that time of day. Worse still, the weather grew hazy for several days, taking away even this navigational aid. It was getting hotter, and my load felt heavier with every step. After some uncomfortable wanderings in the valley, I decided to make my way back to the seaside and my post, then return the same way I'd come.

In this journey my dog surprised a young goat, which I managed to save from his jaws. If I could bring it home, it would further my goal of raising a herd of tame goats. I made the little creature a collar, and with some light rope that I always carried, I led him home with me. I brought him inside my enclosure and forgot about him for the moment, for I was very impatient to relax. I had been gone almost a month, and I was deeply tired of traveling. How satisfying to lie down in my hammock! I decided not to venture too far from home again.

I rested for a week, spending most of my time making a cage for my bird, who began to grow friendlier toward me. I regret to say that I neglected the little goat for a couple of days, until he began to bleat pitifully with hunger. I cut some branches and grass for him, and threw these into the enclosure. Soon I had no need to tie him up—he became so friendly and gentle that he followed me around like the dog (whom I had to teach, with no small trouble, that this goat was not supper). Some company was better than none at all.

In time the fall rainy season arrived, and I kept the 30th of September in the same solemn manner as before. Now I began to be more grateful for my life as it was. My old, selfish, wicked life was a thing of the past. God had provided me with all I needed, including the time to reflect on my errors. In the past two years, I had been prone to sudden bouts of deep sorrow, where I would weep like a child. At those times, I saw myself as a prisoner, and I would vent my grief with words and tears until it was spent. My daily Bible readings were a great source of comfort.

One sad morning I had opened the Scriptures to these words: "I will never, never leave thee, nor forsake thee." These words seemed designed just for me; why else should I find them at just that moment of mourning? "Well, then," said I, "if God does not forsake me, who cares if the rest of the world does? I am better off."

At that moment I had begun to decide I could be happier here than anywhere in the world, but something rang false. "How can you be such a hypocrite?" I demanded of myself. "Pretend to be as content as you like, but in honesty, you would pray heartily to be delivered from here. If a Spanish ship came along this afternoon, you would go to insane lengths to get its attention, and weep like a child if you didn't succeed." On this second anniversary, I remembered that conversation with myself, and adopted a more rational view. I couldn't honestly thank God for my lonely confinement, but I could thank Him for opening my eyes to my past and providing for me here and now. In this frame of mind, I began my third year.

My typical day began with Scriptural reading and prayer, which I did twice more before sleeping again. I hunted in the mornings, or butchered and preserved what I had. During the hottest part of the day, I rested in the shade. Sometimes I labored at projects, such as making boards for shelves—no slow task when one must cut down the tree, remove the limbs, and saw lumber from it. Two sawyers with a full set of tools could have made six boards in a day, whereas I achieved a tiny fraction of a board in one day's work. I describe this so that the reader may not think I spent long hours in laziness; as I ought to know, the need to live better can inspire great heights of industry.

By November and December, I was expecting my first solid crop of barley and rice. The ground I had manured and dug up for them was relatively small, for I had little seed. Now that I had made peace with the weather, and my grain was growing nicely, I found I was in danger of losing it all in other ways. It was very hard to keep goats away from it, as well as rabbits, both of which would graze a stalk down to the soil. There was no solution but to build a fence, which I did, putting the dog on guard duty at night inside. After awhile, the hungry land animals left my crop alone.

I rejoiced until the birds moved in, coming in a great flock to feast on my hard work. I couldn't guard it at all hours, nor could I shoot them all. I fired a shot to scare them away, then went among the stalks to see what damage had been done. A good deal was ruined, but the rest might be saved. The thieves were waiting in the trees all around me, prepared to resume their meal as soon as I left. Sure enough, the moment I went away the feathered bandits returned to feeding. I was furious and frustrated. In my anger, I shot three of them dead, and then I got an inspiration. In England, hanged thieves and pirates were often left on display to discourage others. I collected the dead birds and hung them up as scarecrows, and the result was like magic. Not only would the rest not come near, they abandoned my part of the island. My crop was saved.

By late December, it was time to harvest. Lacking any sickle or scythe, the best tool available to me was one of the ship's broad cutlasses. I got nearly two bushels of rice, and two and a half of barley, or so I guessed. At least with my surplus of cats, I could store this in my cave without fear of rodents befouling it. Now I could hope for the day when I might have bread. That is, if I could figure out how to husk my grain, grind it to flour, then bake it—none of which I knew the least thing about. I turned my thoughts to this process, hoping to have a plan in place by the time I had a crop to process. Few people truly realize the many tasks that go into the making of a simple loaf of bread, but I would have to master them all in some way.

CHAPTER 8

A Boat

*I*f I wanted a proper supply of bread, I would have to plow up more land. I now had enough seed to plant an acre, but my shovel was wearing out. I spent a week making a new one before spading up two large flat pieces of ground near my house. After planting, I fenced these in with that same willowy stakes as before, confident that they would turn into a living hedge.

This work spanned three months but did not actually take all that time, for part of it was the wet season. While confined, I amused myself trying to teach my parrot to speak. I named him "Poll," and when he learned to say his name, it was the first word I heard spoken on the island by a mouth not my own.

A pottery project then took up most of my time, for I had to think ahead. If I got a great crop, where would I put it all? I knew where to find some clay, and I thought the sun might dry pots for me—perfect for grain, flour, and such. I decided to make two great earthen jars. Kind reader, if you could have seen my early efforts, you would have either pitied me or laughed at me. What odd, ugly, misshapen things I made! Making large clay pots is very difficult without a pottery wheel. Many fell in, or out, or cracked in the heat, or fell apart the moment I picked them up—most frustrating.

All this clay, of course, had to be dug up and hauled home from wherever I found it. In the end, it took me two months and countless failures to make two large ugly earthen containers—calling them "jars" would give them too much credit. I made two big wicker baskets around these, to help prevent them from breaking. Hopefully they would hold my grain, and eventually my flour. I did better with smaller items, such as little round pots, flat dishes, pitchers, and such, a supply of which I manufactured in between large container failures.

What I wanted most, though, was a way to heat liquid. No sun-dried clay vessel would take the fire's heat. This problem was solved by sheer luck one day after I was done cooking some meat. As I went to douse the fire, I found a broken piece of my pottery (perhaps one I had thrown in frustration) in the ashes and embers. The piece was baked to a stony red finish. If one piece would bake thus, perhaps a whole vessel might.

But how to set up my fire for this? I had no notion of a kiln, as potters use, nor of glazing them with lead. I did know that the idea was to surround the items with intense heat. So I put three decently sized pots in a pile, one atop another, on top of my embers. I then built up firewood all around the stack and even on top, and kept the fire well fed. Soon the clay vessels were red-hot, but not cracking, and I kept them that way about six hours—until the sand mixed with the clay actually began to melt. Then I let the fire slacken. I had to tend it all night, lest it decline too quickly, but in the morning I had three good (if not handsome) earthen pots that would sit safely over any fire I might build. The molten sand had even glazed one of them with an appealing shine.

Now I could make functional pottery. It wasn't very pretty, for my shaping methods had much in common with children making mud pies, but no one was ever so overjoyed over such a crude success. It took all my patience to wait for them to cool before setting one on the fire to boil some meat. It worked! I had an excellent meal of boiled goat and broth that evening.

With storage solved, I turned to other parts of the bread process. To pound my grain to flour, I needed a stone mortar. My grindstone could be made to sharpen axes, but not to grind grain. I had absolutely no knowledge of the stonecutter's trade, nor any of the necessary tools, but I gave it a try. I spent many days seeking a great stone that I might hollow into a mortar, but my best candidate was of the same sandy rock as all the other rocks on the island. It tended to crumble, and I soon saw that in practical usage it would contaminate my flour with sand.

If stone wouldn't work, perhaps wood might. I found a great block of hard wood, which I pushed and rolled back to my home. After shaping its outside with my axe and hatchet, I employed a clever method used by Brazil's Indians to make canoes. I built a small fire atop it, tending it carefully so that it might burn its way inside without harming the outside. I completed the hollowing with a hatchet, then made a great heavy pestle of ironwood. When their turn came, these tools served me well.

How might I sift the husks from my flour? I really needed a sieve, but of course I had none. I might use coarse cloth, but I had precious little of any sort of cloth. The best remedy I found was among the seamen's clothes I had salvaged: some neck cloths of calico or muslin, with which I made three small sieves that would let the fine flour through. These served my need for some years.

Baking would present another obstacle. I had no yeast, so no point in worrying about it. I also had no oven, and that I must worry very much about. After long consideration, I thought I might make some clay baking covers and a hearth-stone. I shaped wide, shallow clay boxlike covers two feet across but only nine inches deep. I gave them long handles, the longest I thought would hold together, then fired these and set them aside to cool. These would cover my loaves. The hearthstone was easier; I simply made and fired a great clay slab. When baking time came, I built a huge fire. When the firewood burned down to embers or live coals, I piled them on top of my hearth to get it very hot. Then I swept the coals aside, set my loaves in their place, and covered them with my baking covers. After that it was just a matter of piling the hot coals all around the covers, and soon I was baking fine (if unleavened) barley loaves. I even became a good pastry cook, though I never got so far as to make meat pies.

All this took most of my third year on the island. In between, of course, I had my crops to manage. With no need to process all the grain at once, I stored most of it in large baskets, pots, and so on. When I needed more flour, I would grind and sift some rice or barley. My farming was a fine success, yielding twenty bushels each of rice and barley per year. Now I could now eat all the bread I wished, but I was running out of room to store my grain. I had to expand the cave to accommodate my success. I learned that forty bushels of grain would last me a whole year with-out skimping, so I needed only one crop each year. The fields might lie fallow the rest of the time, and thus recover their fertility.

During this year of focus on farming and bread, I often thought of the mainland. I wanted to go there, and perhaps end my isolation, but I failed to consider the dangers. The fierce Indians of the Caribbean coast might make deadlier enemies than the great cats of Africa. I had heard many stories of Europeans who met with disaster among angry natives, and I ought to have remembered them. For now, I thought only of how to get there.

Too bad I didn't have Xury and the longboat, with which I had sailed a thousand miles of the African coast. I thought of our ship's boat, which had washed well up on shore in the storm, and went down to assess her condition. She lay bottom up against a high sandy ridge along the tide line. With more hands, I might well have righted her very quickly, but she was far too heavy for me. I could no more turn her over than I could remove the island. I cut levers and rollers, in hopes of heaving her upright and repairing any damage. If this could be done, I might sail her wherever I wished.

After a great deal of fruitless heaving, I finally had to dig the sand out below her, setting down wood to guide her when I got her loose. All in vain; even then I could not move her. I would have to find some other way, but now I was keener than ever before to find some way to the mainland.

I got to thinking: might I make myself a canoe? I had seen native canoes in Brazil, and this seemed like a fine idea. While I had fewer hands and skills than a tribe of natives, I had more modern tools. Did I think the matter all the way through to a successful launch? Ha! Not I. Intoxicated with the notion, I never once considered that it might be easier to paddle it over a hundred miles of sea than to drag it over a hundred yards of land in order to reach the sea to begin with.

No, I went to work upon this boat like the greatest fool in the history of man. I delighted in my plans and design, and when I did think of launching it, I dismissed such petty concerns: "When it's done, I'll find a way to move it." I began by felling a cedar tree, and I doubt Solomon himself ever had such a great timber for the building of the Temple of Jerusalem. It was nearly six feet wide at the base, and twenty feet up the trunk it was still five feet wide. I spent five weeks cutting it down, then limbing it. The work of shaping its bottom into a boatlike form took me another month. To clear out the inside took three more months of carefully controlled fires, supplemented by mallet and chisel. What a task!

I was tremendously proud of the result—at first, anyway. My handsome canoe would have carried twenty-six men, or me and all my cargo. Had I gotten it into the water, I would have promptly begun an insane voyage. As it was, I had absolutely no way to launch my craft. It was one hundred yards from the creek, and a small hill intervened between boat and the logical launch site.

Now what? I decided to dig into the earth, cutting a canal from the stream to my canoe. It would take a tremendous effort, but who worries about effort with deliverance in sight? After a few days of fatiguing toil, I got to calculating, and estimated that this process would take me as much as ten or twelve years. With great reluctance, I abandoned this doomed project.

In the middle of this work, I completed my fourth year of solitude. I kept the anniversary with devotion and gratitude, for my faith had given me a fresh perspective. I felt apart from the world; there was nothing to covet, little opportunity for sin except for blasphemous thoughts and words. I might call myself a king or an emperor; it would not have changed a thing. I could have raised shiploads of grain, but I had no use for such amounts, and raised only what I needed. I had enough turtles to feed many, but there was no point in killing more than one at a time, and that only occasionally. I had enough timber to build a small fleet, and enough grapes to load that fleet with a fine cargo of raisins—for all the good it would have done me.

At the same time, I could use all that was valuable. With enough to eat and supply my wants, what did I care for the rest? If I killed more meat than the dog and I could eat, the rest would simply spoil. Cut down too many trees, and they would lie there to rot. I could only eat so many raisins. I learned a thing: all the good things of this world are only useful to us in the amount we can benefit from them, and beyond that they have no value. My life would have cured the world's greediest miser of his vice. What I had, I had plenty of; what I lacked I could not get for any money. My parcel of gold and silver? It lay sorry and useless. I would have given it all for some tobacco pipes, or a hand mill to grind my grain, or a small bag of turnip and carrot seeds, or better still some peas and beans—even a bottle of ink. As it was, it lay moldering in the damp of my cave. A fortune in diamonds would have met the same result.

My mind and body had both grown comfortable. I ate my meals in thankfulness. I looked more on the bright side of my condition, and less on the dark. I thought less of what I missed, and more of what I enjoyed. This time taught me why most people are discontented: rather than appreciate what God has provided, they lament for what He has not given them. All our unfulfilled desires spring from lack of thankfulness.

The most obvious example of this was the ship. What if it had broken up completely, or not been shifted so close to shore? I might have been without weapons or tools. What then? I would have lived more primitively than any native, if indeed I lived at all, for I lacked their resourceful knowledge. Only my tools and weapons could compensate for my ignorance of survival skills. I imagined myself starving, naked, barely able to kill a goat for my food, and then having to tear it apart with my teeth and fingers. I was far better off than that, and I felt very grateful. Nearly any situation, no matter how miserable, can easily be worse.

My own life before the shipwreck surely bore all this out. My mother and father had tried their best to teach me Christian virtues, but I fell in with blasphemous sailors, and adopted their hardened ways. I had escaped from Sallee, been rescued by the Portuguese captain, found my feet in Brazil, and received my cargo from England; never once had it occurred to me to thank God. I had mentioned Him only to take His name in vain. Yet even now, after more than a man's share of greed and sin, it seemed that my repentance had been accepted. My harvest was rich. My home was cool in the heat and dry in the rain. If I felt forgiven, who could blame me?

I even became thankful for my solitude. Neither man nor beast threatened me. I felt like the recipient of a miracle.

Just as well, for many of the supplies from the ship were gone or running out. I eked out my ink with water until it grew too faint to read. The ship's biscuit ran out soon after the ink, leaving me on short rations until I was able to make my own bread. My clothes began to decay; underwear wore out swiftly, and the main clothing I had was seamen's shirts and watch coats. This was a problem because the weather was often violently hot. I didn't want to go naked, for reasons of ingrained modesty and horrible sunburn, but I also didn't want to wear a heavy coat in such punishing heat. I was most comfortable in a light shirt, and my supply of these was falling to rags. What to do?

I had to do something. All my waistcoats were worn out; I must try and convert the watch coats to jackets, using such materials as I had. I set to work tailoring, and did a pitiful job, but I did manage to make three new waistcoats of a sort. I hoped they would last a long time. As for pants and underpants, I had first little and then nothing, wearing my holey rags until they fell off my body.

I dared not neglect hats, for the sun burned down terrifically on my poor head. When I went out in the sun bareheaded, I got a terrible headache. I had a few hats, but they would not last forever and were not well suited to all weather and work conditions. I had, of course, saved the skins of every four-footed creature I killed, stretching them with sticks in the sun. Some had grown dry and hard, but others were very useful. My first leatherwork was a great goatskin cap for my head, with the hair outward, to keep off the rain. This worked so well that I made a suit of the same material: a waistcoat and pants open at the knees, both very loose so that I could keep cool. While I was an even worse tailor than I was a carpenter, they kept off the rain and were comfortable in hot weather. I could ask no more.

Next I thought I should have an umbrella, for shelter against both downpours and extreme heat. The first one I made fell apart in the wind; the second lasted only a bit longer. Correcting my mistakes, I managed to make a third that would hold together. It would open well enough, but was very difficult to close. Even so, I could now move more freely even in very wet weather, with less fear of catching another fever.

In all, I lived quite comfortably, having resigned myself to God's will and cast myself on his mercy. When I began to regret the lack of conversation, I would converse with my own thoughts, and (I believed, and hope it was true) with God himself. Surely that should satisfy me more than any human society.

CHAPTER 9

Tames Goats

*T*he next five years were mainly quiet for me. I planted, cured raisins, and hunted. I refined my crafts and kept my devotions. I taught Poll some phrases, kept my country home in good repair, and tried to think of new uses for all the scrap I'd gotten from the wreck years before.

Beyond these basic activities, I had little to do. I decided to get my canoe into the water, which meant I must forge ahead and make the canal after all. The short version of this long tale is that I developed better tools and techniques, and eventually got this work done. I had a water-way six feet wide by four feet deep. The reader might try to imagine the joy I felt when I cut through the last dike of earth and let in the water.

I had given up the idea of sailing to the main-land, but I did want to cruise around my island. What might I find?

The question of rigging, put off for years,

now came to the fore. Fortunately, I still had many spare sails from the ship, and had no trouble stepping a small mast in my canoe with one of these attached. The first sea trials were very promising, so I made little boxes at each end of my boat for provisions and equipment. I cut a long hollow in one side to lay my gun, and hung a goatskin flap over it to keep it dry. I set up a place in the stern to mount my umbrella.

After some small sea trials near the creek mouth, I was ready for a voyage of discovery. I stocked my boxes with two dozen loaves (more accurately, barley cakes), a pot of rice, a little bottle of rum, some salted goat, powder and shot, and two large watch coats: one to lie on, the other to cover me at night. The day was November 6, in the sixth year of my reign—or my captivity, if you prefer. I set sail in high excitement, counterclockwise around the island from the southern shore, with little notion of danger.

While the island was not very large, its east coast had a great, mostly submerged peninsula. It took the form of a rocky shoal, sandy in places, with sandbars and rocks alike breaking the surface here and there. I had not known its exact nature until sailing this near, and it went farther out to sea than I had suspected. At no point could I safely cross the shoals in my canoe—I must go the entire way around the point.

At first I was going to give up and return, but

it seemed a shame to throw away such monumental effort. I anchored my craft in the shallows with a broken grappling hook from the wreck, then took my gun and ventured ashore. A nearby hill delivered a better view of the situation, and I saw that my main obstacle was not the point but a very powerful sea current running north and east near the tip of the shoal. It might well carry me out to sea, with no way to get back. I had also seen this current at the other side of the island, so I must be alert for it. However, there was also a large eddy near the shore on either side of the long shoal. Provided I didn't linger in the current, I should be able to reach this area of conflicting but relatively calm water and continue my travels.

Even so, I lay up here two days, for the wind was blowing pretty hard against the current. I didn't want to try waters where the sea and wind were battling, so I waited. On the morning of the third day, with the wind abated to a light breeze, I put to sea again.

I am a warning to all rash, ignorant boat pilots. No sooner had I come to the point than the current grabbed my boat. I could not get free, and it took all my attention and effort to keep my craft near its edge. I saw the gentle roils of the eddy on my left growing farther away.

With little wind, and my paddles nearly useless, I began to think myself lost. I would be hauled out to sea, where I must eventually starve. I had found a great turtle on shore while waiting for my opportunity, and I had brought a big jar of fresh water, but who knew when I might reach land again? The mainland was almost precisely the opposite direction. I might perish of thirst before I ran out of food.

Now I saw how easily a bad situation could be made far worse. My desolate, solitary island—growing smaller in my vision each moment—felt like the most pleasant place in the world. I wanted only to be there again. I appealed with arms wide:

"My happy desert!" I cried out. "I will never see you again. I am lost! Where will I end up?"

Then I blamed myself, for in the back of my mind, I knew that I was still holding onto some regret over my solitude. What I would have given, right then, to have that same loneliness back! We never properly value a thing until it is taken away from us.

I despaired but didn't surrender. I kept my boat angled landward, hoping to reach the eddy, and about noon I thought I felt a little breeze. This cheered me a little, and more when it built into a mild gale. By this time I had been carried a frightful distance from my island, and it was a good thing there were no heavy clouds or haze, or I might have lost all sight of the island. As it was, I spread my sail again to catch the breeze.

Just as I had my sail oriented, and was making headway toward the current's edge, I saw a change in the water. I had reached a shallow place that interrupted the current. My canoe skipped into the eddy. Those who have been saved from imminent hanging, or rescued from murderous thieves, can imagine my joy.

The eddy carried me some distance back toward the island, far north of where the current had captured me. I soon saw the shoreline curving around to the island's northern side. The breeze came and went, but I was able to make decent progress. By early evening I dropped my makeshift anchor in a peaceful little cove.

When I was on shore, I fell on my knees and thanked God for my deliverance. I gave up on the notion of escaping my island by boat. I wasn't even sure I could sail the entire way around it, but that question would wait until tomorrow. After getting something to eat and drink, exhaustion gave swift way to sleep.

The next morning I had to confront the crucial question: how should I go home? I was most reluctant to try the east coast again, but I had no idea what lay along the west, except that the current resumed somewhere nearby. I decided to watch for a creek mouth or cove along this north coast, as a permanent mooring place for my canoe. Then I would have it again when I wanted it, though not along the mainland side. I would walk home, for I had gotten my fill of seafaring for a while.

After about three miles of sailing I found a very convenient little harbor. When I had my canoe moored, I saw familiar ground about me; I had come this way on foot before. Taking only my gun and umbrella, for it was terribly hot, I began the second to last leg of my travels. I arrived at my country home in the evening to find all in good order as usual, and laid down in the shade to rest my weary limbs.

Try to imagine my surprise when a voice woke me up crying out: "Robin, Robin, Robin

Crusoe! Poor Robin Crusoe! Where are you, Robin Crusoe? Where are you? Where have you been?" At first I only partly awoke, so tired was I from rowing and sailing and walking, thinking it was a dream. The voice kept repeating, "Robin Crusoe, Robin Crusoe," until at last I came wide awake in frightened confusion.

I heard the voice once more and looked that direction. There was my Poll sitting on top of the hedge, perfectly delighted with himself. He had learned to perch on my arm and cry, "Poor Robin Crusoe! Where are you? Where have you been? How did you come you here?" and the like. Even after realizing it was only the parrot, it took me some time to compose myself. I was amazed that he had come looking for me, and comforted by his presence, so I called him by name. He flew over and sat on my arm, as usual, keeping up the same sort of talk. In the morning, when I started for my hillside home, he rode on my shoulder in his usual way.

On that march, I reflected quite a bit. I would have been glad to bring my boat back around to my side of the island, but my blood ran cold when I remembered my experience off the eastern coast. What if the current were as strong off the west coast—or even stronger? The more I considered this, the more I endorsed my decision to leave the boat along the north, no matter how many tedious years I'd spent getting it to sea. I knew the way home well, of course, and was soon back to my usual sedate life.

The next year or so was quite happy for me, if you discount the lack of human company. I developed into a fairly skilled carpenter, especially considering my limited selection of tools, and with this skill I contrived a potter's wheel. Now my pottery was round and uniform, not formless and lumpy. I managed to create and fire a clay tobacco pipe, which I smoked now and then, for this had been a habit of mine. My basket-weaving also showed improvement, though it would always be more functional than handsome. Smaller baskets were ideal for transporting goat meat and skins, or turtle eggs and flesh; larger ones held part of my stored grain.

Too bad I couldn't grow gunpowder and shot, for both were slowly running out. The day would come when I must reserve the remainder for emergencies. I pondered how I might hunt, but then thought: why not arrange it so that I need not hunt at all? The tame nanny goat I had brought home had died a spinster at a comfortable old age. By my eleventh year in residence, I began studying safe ways to trap goats—ideally mostly female, and pregnant if possible.

I began with snares, but they didn't work. I always found them broken or chewed and my barley-ear bait gone. I tried pit traps covered with thin frameworks of branches, but these didn't fool the goats for a long time. You might wonder why I had such a hard time getting this art right. The explanation is simple: I could only go by the evidence (if any) the goats left as they raided or avoided my traps.

Finally, after many refinements and much frustration, I went one morning to check my pit traps. One contained a large old billy goat in a very ill temper. In another were three kids: a male and two females. Perfect!

The old billy was so fierce I doubted he would ever be a tame herd member. I dared not go down to get him; those who think goats are harmless have never jumped down in a hole with a large, infuriated one. I didn't want to kill him, so I spent considerable time throwing a rope down until I got it around him. When I managed to drag him out, bleating in outrage, he ran off as if a lion were chasing him. I had forgotten an important fact: hunger will tame nearly any animal. Had I merely left him down there, and just given him water to drink and then a little grain, he might have calmed down, for goats are very mild creatures when treated kindly.

The kids were easier to manage, and one by one I climbed down to get them. I tied my little group together and led them home, in hopes that they would form the start of a fine herd. At first they wouldn't feed, but they soon got hungry enough to eat the grain I put out for them. But how might I keep the wild goats out and the tame goats confined? I needed to fence some pasture.

I couldn't just build a fence at any random place. The location must have plenty of grazing, a ready source of water, and some form of shade. I knew of a fine open meadow with two or three little springs of fresh water, and woods at one end. My first plan was to build an enclosure roughly two-thirds of a mile across. Those who know anything of fence building will immediately calculate that this meant two miles of fencing, but what else did I have to do? I could have enclosed five times as much ground, but I needed to be able to chase and catch them.

After cutting and planting about fifty yards of hedge, I decided to start smaller. An area about 150 yards by 100 would do to begin with, and if my herd outgrew this, I could always fence more pasture. In the three months it took me to hedge this area, I kept the kids tied in the best part of it, always near me. Often I hand-fed them some ears of barley or handfuls of rice, so they would learn that I was their friend. Even after I finished the fencing and set them loose, they would follow me up and down, bleating for a treat.

In about a year and a half I gathered and bred a herd of twelve goats, kids and all. In two more years I had forty-three, and had begun to slaughter one now and then for food. After that,

I enclosed five more such pastures, with little pens to corral the goats when I wanted, and gates to get between pastures. I could salt any meat I butchered, using salt dried from seawater, but what pleased me most was the dairy.

I only thought of this when I saw the first batch of newborn kids nursing. I had never milked even a cow in my life, much less a goat, but I soon learned the method. Before long I had a gallon or two of milk per day. After much trial and error, I learned to make butter and cheese: what utter delights! How generous our Creator, to provide for my wants in such a way! What a table was spread for me in the wilderness, where I saw nothing at first but death by hunger!

CHAPTER 10

Find a Man's Footprint in the Sand

*M*y friends in England or Brazil would have smiled to see my little family sit down to dinner. His Majesty, lord of the whole island, held absolute power over his subjects. I had the power to bind and to loose, to kill and to spare. My subjects never rebelled. And indeed I dined like a king, attended only by my retainers! Poll the parrot was the only subject permitted to speak to me. My dog, now a senile, old bachelor, sat on my right. A cat sat on each side of my table, each expecting a treat now and then as a mark of royal favor.

These, of course, were not the cats I had brought ashore. I had given both of those little burials near my home. One had somehow found other felines to breed with, and their descendants ran wild in the woods. Only these two had I managed to tame, and that was enough company; the rest raided my food so persistently I had to start shooting them on sight. These two I had chosen for their friendly natures, and the rest soon learned to leave me alone.

With much time for my nerves to recover from my near disaster at sea, I began to think of using my boat again. How to do so without running foolhardy risks? I tried to think up a way to get her back to my side of the island. Over time, eagerness began to win out over caution, and one day I decided to go have another good look at the long eastern shoal.

On this march, as I often did, I smiled at the figure I would cut back home in Yorkshire. It may please the reader to sketch me. Here is what you would draw:

Begin with a man with a great shapeless, hairy cap, with a flap hanging behind to keep the sun and rain from his neck. About his body is a shaggy goatskin jacket reaching to his thighs. He wears short pants, not quite to the knees, so hairy that from a distance it appears he might be wearing a skirt. He has no regular shoes and no stockings at all, but neither is he quite barefoot; he has leather buskins laced up his calves with heavy thongs.

Your artistic subject is well enough equipped. He wears a broad goatskin belt, from which dangle a saw and a hatchet. Over his shoulder is a narrower belt with two pouches hanging from it: one for powder, the other for shot. On his back is a wicker basket held by shoulder straps. In his right hand is a musket; in the other is a great, clumsy, ugly goatskin umbrella—closed or open, as you prefer.

As for my face, it had not grown quite as tan as you might expect, but more so than your typical Englishman. I had once let my beard grow partway down my chest, but these days I kept it fairly short; the same for the hair on my head. My mustache, however, was a monstrous thing. Draw it very bushy, drooping far down on either side of my mouth. In England, of course, I would have been a fright—but with no one present to mock my appearance, I hardly needed to care what anyone might think.

When I reached the spot where I'd anchored before my ill-fated voyage, I went up the hill to observe the shoal. To my surprise, there was no violent current. I was at a total loss to explain this, and decided to spend some time observing its patterns. In evening I went up again and saw that the current was back, only further out to sea than the one I had experienced. Most likely it was the combination of natural tides and the varying power and direction of the wind, perhaps influenced by some large river emptying from the nearby mainland. If so, I could easily bring my boat around the island by making prudent observations of the tides.

It is one thing to think, however, and quite another to dare. I will admit that my healthy respect for the current was mixed with a fair bit of remembered terror. I wasn't able to overcome this, so I came to a safer but more laborious resolution: I would build another canoe, one for each side of the island. As always: much work, but I had little else to do. My hard work on home building and improvement was largely done, as I saw it. My cave was quite large enough, my wall secure; in fact, this had taken root and grown tall, with limbs spread wide and tangled above me. At any distance at all, an observer would see it only as another clump of trees. A little inland and below my home were my two grainfields, which I planted and tended in season. If I needed a greater crop, I could plow up more land.

At my country home, the circle of stakes had likewise grown into a thick hedge. I had pruned them so that their branches and leaves spread completely over the middle. My tent was a piece of sail spread over poles, and had held up well. I had made a sort of low couch from animal skins stuffed with straw and dried grass, and I kept a blanket and a large watch coat there.

My goat pastures were fairly near this area, and I had continually enhanced the fencing until the sprouted trees were almost like a palisade—I had actually had to remove some. My farming enabled me to subsist; herding goats allowed me to feast. Here also grew my grapes, most of which I stored up as raisins for the rainy seasons.

Now I went to this country home, the nearest

to my boat. From time to time I had gone to the harbor to check on my boat, sometimes going on brief cruises very close to shore. I took no chances of being hurried out to sea by current, wind, or other accident. I was preparing for one of these little boat outings when I saw the sight that divided my life on the island.

Before me was a human footprint. There was no mistaking it; the print was deep and clear in the moist sand.

I stood as if I'd seen a ghost. I listened and looked round me, but I could neither see nor hear anything. I went up and down the shore in search of others, but there were none—just this lone print of a human foot.

How had it gotten there? My mind rummaged for explanations, all in a great stir of confusion. I hurried home to my castle (which I had begun to call my primary home), looking behind me every few steps. I suspected every bush and every tree. All the norms of my life were overturned. My head was full of strange frights, imagined dangers, and weird plans of action. I don't even remember whether I went through the cave door or scrambled over the ladder; I fled inside as though an entire tribe of angry natives were after me. No frightened rabbit ever bolted for cover in greater terror.

I didn't sleep at all that night. My distance from the spot where I saw the footprint gave me

no solace at all, contrary to the usual nature of such things. A part of me was deeply embarrassed at my panicky reaction, but I covered this up with dismal and irrational ideas as to what it meant. Could it have been the footprint of Satan himself? How else could a human shape come to this place, yet make only one footprint? If a person had made it, where was the vessel that brought him (or her)? Why no other footprints?

Finally I came to my senses. Why would Satan take human shape in such a place, for no other reason than to leave a lone footprint, in a place where I might or might not even find it? If the Devil wanted to terrify me, he could have found far better ways; we normally think of Satan as being much subtler and cleverer in his evil. The elements would eventually wash it away in any case. Thus reassured a bit, I cast aside this line of fearful thinking.

A human, then—but who? Perhaps a canoe full of natives had been blown out to sea, gone briefly ashore, decided against staying on a desolate island, then gone back home as soon as possible. If so, it was a good thing I hadn't been nearby. Surely they hadn't spotted my boat, for if they had, they would have recognized its foreign (and probably, in their eyes, inferior) manufacture. They might well have launched a full-scale search for me. They would surely be skilled trackers, and never in my life had I needed to learn to cover my trail. Even if I managed to hide, they could easily find my fields and my goat pasture, and they might vent their frustration on my food sources. I might have to start all over, if in fact I could.

In my fear and vivid imagination, I forgot all my confidence in the Almighty. It should have been obvious to me that a God who could provide me with such bounty also had the power to preserve it for me. I faulted myself for laziness, for growing only the grain I needed, not thinking of what I might do if my crop were lost. In the future I planned to maintain two or three years' supply of grain, in case of a crop failure or other agricultural disaster.

How strange is the life of man! Today we love what tomorrow we hate; today we seek what tomorrow we shun; today we desire what tomorrow we fear. At no time was this clearer to me. My only sorrow was that I was completely cut off from mankind, my fate a mystery to all who had known me. I would have considered human company the greatest blessing Heaven could bestow, a completion of my happiness. Now I was ready to slink behind trees and hide in a cave at the very thought.

When I had recovered a little, I began to come back to the rock of my faith. If God had put me here, He wanted me here. His was the right to punish or reward. I must not dispute His sovereignty, and if I had sinned, I must bear the consequences. All I could do was have faith and try to live as the Bible said. This view was the product of some weeks of turbulent thought, but it gave me solace and purpose.

In the shorter term, I wondered if the footprint might have been merely my own, somehow isolated. I considered that if that were the case, then I had been like the people who try to frighten others with tales of ghosts, yet are frightened of the random noise in the night more than anybody.

After three days of fearful confinement, I began to take courage. Well I might, for I was running out of barley cakes and water. My goats needed milking, which I usually did in the evenings, and indeed the poor nannies were in great pain due to my inattention. If I weren't careful, their milk might dry up—they could even get sick. So I went out to my milking, repeating to myself that it was just one of my own footprints, as if that would make it certain. My repetitions didn't fully convince my mind, however, to judge by the way I looked behind me and watched every tree and boulder, always ready to drop my basket and run for my life. If there had been another human watching me, he would surely have observed that I must have some terrible sin on my conscience.

Two or three days of normal milking and

farming emboldened me. I was beginning to think I had simply imagined the footprint. I couldn't resist the urge to see the print one more time. If it were still there, a quick comparison would show whether it was mine or not. I had to have the answer, and down I went.

The footprint was still there, but it provided me no comfort whatsoever. In the first place, I knew I hadn't disembarked from my boat at that spot. In the second, it was much larger than my own foot. Back came the flood of imagined dooms and disasters, and I shook like a fevered person. Having ruled out all other explanations, both the rational and the fanciful, only two possibilities remained. Either some man or men had visited, or someone else lived here. I might not be sole lord and master of all I surveyed!

In either case, one day I might be taken by surprise. I had no idea how to prevent this.

In moments of terror, the fertile human brain can propose some of its very silliest notions. My first thought was to demolish all my structures and enclosures, turn my goats loose, and abandon my fields: remove every trace of my residence, so no one would imagine I lived here. What nonsense! The fear of danger is ten thousand times more terrifying than seeing the actual danger firsthand. I prayed and prayed, as I ought to have done more often through this process, instead of waiting for my brain to sort itself out.

This confusion kept me awake until the twilight before sunrise, at which time I fell into exhausted slumber.

When I finally woke up, I had calmed down a great deal. After some internal debate, I reached a new conclusion. This island was pleasant, fertile, and near the mainland. Even if I were the only resident, people might visit for a number of reasons. They might come for grapes, or be blown here by adverse conditions, perhaps even think it a grand adventure. Either way, all I really needed was a safe plan of retreat in case they showed up.

Now I was very sorry I had created a second entrance through my cave, and I decided I must fix this. I began to construct a second wall of earth, stakes and timber, a short way outside my hut. By tramping it down, I packed the earth very tightly, and in this wall I made seven holes at equal intervals—one for each musket that was still in working order. I could thus fire all seven guns at any intruders, without risk to myself, in two minutes' time. The work took many weary months, but I felt unsafe until it was done.

Even then I wasn't satisfied. Far out from this second wall I planted a great many stakes in a dense pattern, the willowy ones I knew would take root. In time they would grow to an impenetrable thicket. In five or six years my reinforced castle was completely hidden by this grove, which would serve as a severe obstacle to any invaders. I left myself only one winding, confusing way in, with many dead ends and looping back on itself, not even easy to spot unless someone knew it was there. And if anyone did get through, whether by cleverness or by determined cutting, I would have clear room to shoot if necessary.

In the end, my measures weren't entirely paranoid, though at the time they were the result of undefined fears.

CHAPTER 11

A Cave Retreat

I needed to secure my castle, to be sure, but my food supply was also vulnerable. Thanks to my herd of goats, I rarely had to hunt and had less need for meat in any case; they provided leather for clothing and other necessaries. Losing my herd would be a disaster, and I spent many hours thinking up ways to protect it.

One method would be to dig an underground cave, and stable the goats there each night. Possible, but a great nuisance to myself and the goats, and the digging would take a long time. I might instead hedge against disaster by dividing my herd. If I were to fence two or three small pastures elsewhere, with half a dozen young goats in each place, a disaster befalling the main flock would not wipe them all out. It would take a good deal of time and effort, but it made good sense to me.

I searched the island for promising locations.

The best spot, oddly enough, was in the middle of the same valley where I had once wandered lost. This little meadow was hemmed in with woods, and would require less effort to enclose than other places; it had water. In a month's time I had it well enough fenced to secure ten young nannies and two billies. While I perfected the fence, they could get used to their new residence.

All this labor and worry because of a single human footprint.

Two years passed. Still I did not see another actual human, but I was never at ease. Even my religious habits were affected. In the recent past, my prayers had been sedate and grateful; at this point they were full of fearful pleas for security. Every night I wondered if I might be murdered before morning, and my tone with the Almighty reflected this.

After I had established my first reserve goatherd, I sought the site for another. This took me further west on the island than I had ever before gone. As I looked out to sea, I thought I saw a boat in the distance. Had I carried one of the ship's spyglasses, I might have known more, and I resolved to carry one in the future.

As I came down to the southwestern shore, I decided that a man's footprint was not such a strange thing at all. I had simply had the good fortune to wash ashore on the natives' least favorite side of the island. Perhaps they only came here as a safe haven in case of trouble at sea. I knew that some native groups actually fought sea battles with others in canoes; maybe, for whatever reason, they brought their prisoners here.

I was about to learn one of those reasons. I saw some debris on the beach a short distance away and went to investigate. What a horror!

The shore was spread with skulls, hand bones, foot bones—indeed, every sort of bone in the human body. Near all this was a fire pit, where some of the bones' original owners had perhaps been roasted for dinner.

Cannibalism! I knew it was possible, but to see actual evidence was a profound shock. In my horror and nausea I forgot even my own security; I became violently ill on the spot. When I finished vomiting, my stomach felt better but not my soul.

I hurried homeward. Some distance inland, I stopped and recovered a bit. With a flood of tears, I thanked God for many things: not having been born among cannibals, having come ashore in a safe place where I could establish myself, and all my comforts and good fortunes, which surely outweighed the irritants and mishaps.

In this frame of mind I went home to my castle, and indeed I felt safer then. The visitors apparently didn't venture inland, or sometime in these eighteen years our paths would have crossed. Everything I owned was well camouflaged. With due caution, I might well be left alone for another eighteen years. Unless I found natives who did not eat human flesh—a distinct possibility—I did not intend to be found.

Thus, for the next two years, I rarely ventured outside my establishments: my castle, my country home, and my fields and pastures. I went nowhere near my boat during this time, for I had lost all interest in seafaring. At sea I was at my most vulnerable.

As time wore on, I resumed most of my old and sedate ways—but not all. I kept a closer eye out now, to see others before they saw me, and I made less noise. Thanks to my goatherd, I had no need to shoot; I could kill turtles without guns, and I learned to set traps and snares for wild goats. I always went armed with pistols and an old cutlass, but I doubt I fired a single shot in those two years. If you sketched me earlier, you may add these weapons to your portrait of Robinson Crusoe.

I did a lot of thinking in those two nervous years. What concerned me most, after the chance of capture, was the disgusting notion that people might eat human flesh within a few miles of me. After many years of experimenting and inventing in the name of my own comfort and security, I turned my creative side to a harsher motive: the desire to punish some of the cannibals in the act, and to save their victims if I could.

It would take a much longer book to detail all the notions I discarded. I must be nearby in order to take any action, which would put me within range of well-aimed arrows and blowgun darts. Either might be poisoned. From my time in Brazil I knew that South America's natives were fine marksmen with bow and blowgun alike. Might I bury five or six pounds of gunpowder beneath the fire pit? My powder supplies had dwindled to a single barrel, which I could not afford to waste. Even if I did, I could not be sure if or when it would explode. It might only surprise them, and that would be very dangerous in the long run.

In time I decided to lay an ambush. I would hide with an armload of guns, and start shooting only when they were occupied with the meal. If my first volley was good, I might finish them all off with pistols and the cutlass. I often dreamed of this, and went so far as to scout a proper place to lay in wait. This meant several trips down to the coast, where I could not help seeing the fire pit and the bones. My horror and malice grew with each visit. Eventually I discovered a well-concealed hillside perch above the beach, near enough to score hits with double-loaded muskets. I must try to take out at least two enemies with each shot.

When I decided it was time for action, I loaded two muskets with two slugs each plus four or five smaller bullets. To this I added a bird gun, full of the largest shot it could use. The pistols I loaded with four bullets each, useless at long range but that didn't matter—these were for close work, and each shot must count. I brought two reloads for each weapon, and of course I brought the cutlass. Thus bristling with weapons, I nestled in my hiding place and kept watch.

I saw nothing that day, nor the next. Every day I walked the three miles or more to my ambush point and watched. No one.

After two or three fruitless months without a single sighting, I started to get bored. With a great deal of time to ponder, I began to ask myself: what right had I to play judge and executioner? Heaven had not punished them in many ages; why might I? What had they done to me? They did not consider it a crime, no worse than I thought of slaughtering a goat.

And were my European relatives necessarily better? Were Christians murderers when they put battle captives to the sword? What of the millions of native people killed in the New World by Spanish soldiers? While some of those held to pagan beliefs and conducted bloody rites, they had done the Spaniards no harm at all. Even many Spaniards felt their nation's atrocities had sullied its proud name.

I could no longer justify my plan. If natives attacked me, I had the right to defend myself, but

I could likely avoid them altogether. I had no right to shoot them down in cold blood. The attempt might even be the end of me. What if even one escaped to tell his comrades? They might come by the thousands to seek just revenge. I decided to return to my policy of hiding, and leave matters of moral justice to God. I knelt to thank Him for delivering me from bloody guilt, and asked His protection, in hope that I might never need to kill a man.

In hindsight, my good fortune was monumental. What if I had discovered not a footprint, but fifteen or twenty visitors—and myself armed only with a single bird gun? I might have been ambushed myself; if I ran, I might have been tracked down. Often we are delivered from danger without even knowing it was there; sometimes we are guided by secret hints, which we only see as divine guidance when we look back. It is never too late to be wise.

A side effect of my policy was the end of new construction. I was afraid to drive a nail or chop wood; what if someone heard me? I was reluctant to build any fire in daytime, lest the smoke betray me. For this reason I relocated to my reserve goat pen in the valley all of my tasks requiring fire, especially making my pottery and baking implements. I chose this location due to a very welcome discovery one day while I was cutting wood. My goal was to make charcoal, which burns with little or no smoke. One can make it by partly burning wood under turf, which likewise conceals most of the smoke. I believed this would help me hide my fires.

While gathering the wood, I happened to notice the entrance to a natural cave concealed behind a bit of underbrush. My curiosity led me inside.

A few feet into the cave, two broad eyes shone out at me! Whether they were some devil, or a man, I didn't wait to see. I ran out much faster than I'd gone in.

After a long interval to recover my courage, I called myself a thousand kinds of fool. Nothing snarled at me, nor came out after me. If I was afraid of a couple of eyes in a cave, I was hardly fit to have lived twenty years here alone. I lit a piece of wood for a torch and went back inside.

As I entered, I heard a loud sigh like a man in pain. Then came a broken noise like a person trying to speak, then another sigh. I broke into a cold sweat. Had I been wearing a hat, my hair might well have lifted it off. Again I plucked up and stepped forward to see.

In front of me lay a very large, old billy goat, apparently dying of old age. Perhaps I had interrupted him in making out his last will and testament. I stirred him a bit, but he couldn't get up. I saw no reason to bother his final moments, so I chose to bypass him and explore this cave further.

It might well be a superb place of retreat.

I was in a chamber that was perhaps twelve feet wide, of irregular shape, with a low passage on the far side. To explore that, I would have to crawl with a candle, of which I had none about me. I decided to continue exploring the next day, better equipped. One invention I haven't yet described was my tinderbox, which I had built around the flint and steel from a broken musket. I had also learned to make very good candles of goat tallow, though I was hard pressed for wicks and used a combination of rags, rope yarn, and dried woven grass.

The next morning I brought my tinderbox and six large candles down to the cave, lit one, and crept inside past the elderly goat. If I may say so, it took me some bravado to creep the ten yards of low passage—but my reward was tremendous.

After crawling that distance, the roof rose to a height of some twenty feet. I stood up to behold the most glorious sight thus far on the whole island: a large chamber studded with something that reflected my candlelight in a thousand spots of glitter. Diamonds? Gold? Crystal? I thought gold the likeliest, but I had no idea. My beautiful new cave had a dry, level floor of loose gravel, with no snakes or any other dangers, nor any damp or wet coming in. The only difficulty was the entrance, but that was part of the appeal. Who could find me here, or harm me if they did?

I was jubilant as I began to consider the possibilities beyond simple refuge. This was the perfect arsenal, so I brought two bird guns and three muskets, leaving five muskets mounted in my outer fence like pieces of cannon. I also relocated most of my remaining bullets and lead. You may remember how one of my powder barrels had been wet from the wreck. I had nearly forgotten about it; now I decided to open it up. The leakage had dried the powder very hard three or four inches in, but this had preserved about sixty pounds of good powder from all conditions. With care I might regrind the hardened part, though sea salt might have spoiled it—I could determine that later. I left only a few pounds of powder at my castle.

Now I fancied myself like one of the ancient giants who was said to live in caves. Here I might lie hidden even with five hundred angry natives combing the island for me. As for the old goat, he died in the cave mouth the next day. To prevent offense to my nose, I dragged him out for burial.

CHAPTER 12

Wreck of a Spanish Ship

I had been on the island twenty-three years. In most ways I was comfortable and well adapted, except for my fear of discovery by hostiles. With prudence, I might have lived happily there until the day when I, like the old goat in the cave, lay down to my final rest.

My animal companions made a great difference. My dog lived sixteen years, and was a loving companion the entire time. I always kept two or three tame cats, getting rid of most of their young and shooting at the wild ones. I also kept two or three household kids at any given time, just for company, and they grew into tame, friendly adult goats.

Poll's speech and general antics were to amuse me for twenty-six years, and after that he may well have lived up to a century for all I know. I caught and tamed two more parrots, but never spent as much time teaching them as I had with

Poll. I also caught several sea birds of unknown breed; when I clipped their wings and fed them, they grew tame. Like the parrots, they nested in the leafy branches of my castle wall; some raised pretty little families, and I made sure none went hungry.

All my needs were met, except for human company. As I'd seen, I might well be careful what I wished for. But how often the thing we fear most becomes our salvation! I could give many examples of this, but the most remarkable came in my last years on the island.

It was December, in my twenty-third year after shipwreck, around the time of the southern solstice. In England we call it the "winter solstice," but to refer to anything on this island as "winter" would be ridiculous. I was up early in the morning, in a fine mood, headed out to harvest my barley.

To my surprise, I saw a fire light on the shore in the distance. I recognized the general area: right where I had found the horrid cooking pit.

I hurried back to my castle, pulled the ladder in and tried to make everything look as natural as possible, but I was a bundle of worries. What if they decided to have a look round the island, and found my neatly planted grain? My buildings? Even my pastures would stand out. No native would be naïve enough to imagine that the trees had randomly grown in nice, orderly rows to enclose a herd of goats. They would want to know who had planted those trees. I loaded all my muskets in their mounts; I checked the priming on my pistols and stuck them into my belt. Asking God's protection and deliverance, I prepared to fight to the last.

The problem with being alone in a battle posture, of course, is that one has no spies to send out. Hungry for information, I climbed up the hillside with a spyglass to see what was happening.

Nine natives were sitting around a small fire on the beach, with three canoes beached near them. They wore nearly nothing. I could think of only one reason they would want fire in such hot weather, and I imagined they might be preparing a barbaric meal at that very moment. With the tide flowing out, perhaps they were awaiting the inbound tide before going away again. If so, this was reassuring: if they preferred to land with the ebb tide, I could go about in safety at other times. I went to my fields to get on with my harvest work, keeping an eye on them from time to time.

Experience proved me right. The natives spent some time dancing about their fire, and when the tide started in again, they boarded canoes and sailed away. The moment they were gone, I armed myself to the teeth: two muskets, two pistols, and my great cutlass. I went down to my old ambush position for a look.

By the time I arrived, their canoes were far out to sea—but the evidence of their visit was not. Blood, bones, and flesh, clearly human, littered the shoreline. The sight sent me straight back to my murderous notions of old. I didn't care how many came next time; I meant to slaughter them all, and I kept a close watch.

But no one else landed—at least not that I knew of. I watched the tides, which was a nuisance when I had no other reason to worry about them. It also was no sure thing, for my notions of their habits did not bind the visitors to a schedule. They could come at any time. Anticipation of misery is worse than the misery itself, especially when one cannot shake it off.

I spent most of the time looking for a way to wipe out the next bunch of cannibals. I could have found much more sensible uses for the time. For some time, of course, I ignored the obvious complications: what if there were two parties? What if some escaped? I would not be able to stop killing once I started. I considered them murderers; well, if I did as I planned, I would soon be a murderer myself—perhaps a far worse one.

I moved about very carefully, always watching and worrying, terrified of capture. How fortunate that I'd thought to herd goats, and had no need to hunt with a musket! A single shot might bring three hundred canoes. My sleep was restless, filled with nightmares. Often I dreamed of killing the intruders—for so I styled them—and how I might justify this act.

One day in May of my twenty-fourth year, as I marked it on the post, a tremendous thunderstorm blew. It lasted well into the night, with great shows of lightning and heavy rains. As I read my Bible, I thought I heard a sound from the dim reaches of my memory: a deep, distant "boom."

I thought for a moment, then remembered. A ship's cannon made that sort of sound.

Of all the surprises I expected from the sea, cannon fire was the least. I hurried to my hilltop just in time to see and hear a second shot, out in the same area where my boat had been driven down the current. It had to be a ship in distress, signaling to another ship for help. I couldn't see the vessel itself, just the flash of the shot.

While I saw no way I could help them, they might well help me. I kept a stock of dry firewood in my cave. When the rain eased for a short time, I hurried to build a bonfire on the hilltop. If there were a ship, and surely there must be, they would see it.

No doubt they did. As soon as my fire blazed up I heard another gun, then several others from the same area. I fed my fire all night, and when the air cleared in the morning, I looked far out to the eastern sea. Through the haze and at such a distance, I could see some sort of large, motionless object.

Might it be a ship at anchor?

You can guess how eagerly I ran down to see. As you will recall, there were rocks far out to sea in that direction, likely invisible to a ship passing in the night. I crested the hill and gazed out along the rocky shoal.

What I saw made me very sad. Upon those rocks hung the wreck of a ship, her masts snapped off near the deck. I saw no motion aboard except for the flapping of tattered sails and ropes. I used my spyglass to search the shoreline for evidence of survivors; no one. Probably all had taken to boats, as my old shipmates had, and been swept off to sea in the same current that had nearly sealed my doom. Or perhaps they had all been evacuated to a sister ship, and gone away—though that would have been extremely perilous in such a storm. Any way one looked at it, their odds were very poor.

Better than most, I knew how their last hours had been. My heart was torn between thankfulness and grief. I felt a great surge of gratitude for my own deliverance; now I was almost surely the lone survivor of two entire ships' companies. I grieved for them, but also for my own loss. Why couldn't at least one or two of them have survived, to be my companions? Never had my loneliness weighed me down so utterly. "Oh, that it had been even one!" I often cried aloud in the days following this event. The human mind is very odd. A desire may remain buried for many years, until some event brings the wish to the surface in a great burst of emotion.

Only a few days later did I learn anything of the crew's fate, and that sadly. I was walking along the shore, gazing at the shipwreck, and came upon a body along the shore. It was a European boy in seaman's clothing, probably the ship's boy. His clothing told me nothing specific about his country of origin. In his pockets were only two pieces of eight and a tobacco-pipe, for which I admit I was most grateful.

With the storm well past, I wanted a closer look at the wreck. The idea of getting something useful was a powerful lure, I admit, but so was that of a survivor clinging to life. Saving him would do everyone good: he would survive, and I would have someone to talk with. I must go, and the sooner the better.

I hastened back to my castle for supplies: barley cakes, a large pot of fresh water, a compass, a bottle of rum, a basket of raisins, rice, the umbrella, a bottle of goat's milk, and a large cheese. I asked God's blessing on my daring voyage, for I had not forgotten what happened before off this coast, and launched my boat once again.

I paddled out to the island's northeast extreme, and here was the point of decision: to venture or not? I looked at the rapid currents, and remembered my terror of old. I might be carried clear out to sea, and never get back again.

For the moment, fear won. I hauled my little boat back to a creek mouth, disembarked and sat down to agonize over my options. With the tide inbound, I dared not go just yet. I decided to climb the small nearby hill for a clear view of the seafaring conditions. From there I saw that the ebb tide's current set out close by the island's south point, meaning that the inbound tide came in hard by the north side. Provided I kept to the north side of the island on my return, I should do well enough. Hopes high, I resolved to set out in the morning. That night I slept under the watch coat in my canoe.

The next day, when I felt the moment was right, I set sail for the wreck. I steered northward out to sea, until I began to feel the eastbound current. This did not take me so swiftly as the southern one had before, and I was still able to paddle and steer. In less than two hours I was alongside the wreck.

A sadder sight you never saw. She was of Spanish manufacture, jammed between two rocks, with her stern and one side beaten in. Her forecastle was damaged; she was dismasted. Only her bow was in decent shape.

I heard a yelping sound and looked up to see a dog at the ship's damaged side rail, whining and barking. Not knowing his name, I called out and gestured encouragement. He braved a leap into the sea—certainly bold but just as certainly desperate—and swam to me. When I got him aboard, I found him almost dead of hunger and thirst. I gave him a cake, which he tore at like a ravenous wolf; as for the water, he would have drunk himself to bursting had I permitted it. Leaving him to recuperate in my canoe, I maneuvered around to the ruined stern where I could easily climb up. I got atop the smashed timbers, tied the canoe to a protruding board, and went on deck.

All was a shambles, of course, but my first truly tragic sight came in the kitchen of the forecastle. There lay two dead men, dressed as typical sailors. By the lack of visible injuries I assumed they must have drowned when high seas broke over the ship and filled the structure with water. I found no one else. The dog and I shared a thing: each of us was a sole survivor. I found no clues, except as I've described, regarding the others' fates.

The seawater had spoiled just about all of the ship's goods. There were some barrels of wine or brandy in the hold, but these were too big to maneuver. I saw several chests, probably belonging to seamen, and got two of these into the boat for later inspection. Going by what I found later when I opened the chests, she might well have been loaded with treasure, but if so it was beyond my reach in the wrecked stern. Perhaps she had sailed from Buenos Aires, or the Rio de la Plata, bound for Havana and eventually her Spanish homeland. As she was, whatever treasure she had aboard was of no use to anyone at that time, me least of all.

I did get a few useful things. With much toil and difficulty, I was able to maneuver a twenty-gallon barrel of rum into my boat. In the cabin was a great powder horn; there were muskets, but of those I already had enough. A fire shovel and tongs were great finds, as were two little brass kettles, a copper pot, and a griddle. I got this much loaded before the tide signaled that it was time to be off, and we made landfall just about an hour after nightfall. I was too exhausted to do anything but go to sleep in my canoe.

On rising, I decided my new goods belonged in my arsenal. With leisure to examine my finds, I opened up the chests and found many good things: a fine case of expensive brandy in bottles, and two well-sealed pots of sweets, some fine shirts, a supply of handkerchiefs and neck cloths, and a great deal of money. Besides three great bags of silver coins—pieces of eight—I found six gold doubloons and about a pound's weight in small gold bars. This must surely have been an officer's chest.

The other chest may have belonged to the gunner's mate, for it held two pounds of fine glazed gunpowder in flasks. In a small bag I also found about fifty pieces of eight, which I would gladly have traded for three or four pair of English shoes and stockings. I had indeed gotten two pair of shoes from the drowned men's feet, but these were different from our English shoes, far less comfortable for my purposes. I laid up the money in my arsenal cave all the same, the thought of what else might lay in the ruined stern flitting through my mind. As I finished my work, I thought that if I ever go back to England, it might still be here until I come back and fetch it.

CHAPTER 13

A Dream Realized

I now sailed my boat back to the hiding spot at her old harbor, then made my way back to my castle. My life was quiet, yet I kept a lookout and was careful of my movements. When I went about, it was usually to the east part of the island, where no visitors ever seemed to come—and where I didn't need an armload of weapons to feel safe. The Spanish ship began to fall apart, subsiding into a shallow watery grave. If it carried any wealth, only I would soon know how to find it.

For the next two years, I bent my mind toward escape. It was my same old weakness: never satisfied with my life, even when it was good. Had I stayed in Brazil, and not gotten so greedy, I might now be a very wealthy gentleman. Instead I went to capture slaves, and wound up here. This passion for escape was foolish, but obviously I hadn't outgrown a lifelong tendency toward foolish passions.

One night during the March rainy season, several months after the shipwreck, I was lying in my hammock thinking of my past and present. In terms of my years on this island, the footprint was the divider, the thing that had altered my basic way of life. I had been comfortable—if blissfully ignorant—before I found it. From the first moment I saw evidence of visitors, I felt unsafe. Likely natives had been visiting the island all along, but so long as I was unaware of that, I had no cares. Sometimes Providence is very kind to us, hiding from our view dangers and worries that would break our spirits.

I wondered how close I had come to disaster. I had been in constant danger. I had blithely fired guns whenever I wished, made all sorts of construction noise, wandered around on the beach, gone on canoe trips mostly to amuse myself. Perhaps nothing but an intervening hill or a clump of trees had saved me more than once. Visitors might kill me with the same lack of remorse I felt when I slaughtered a goat or killed a turtle. I didn't understood how the Lord could allow such a situation, but I did know I ought to be especially grateful to Him for my many years of safety.

My curiosity about these other people was growing. Where did they live? How far off my coast was it? Why did they come this way? Did multiple peoples come here, and might they differ from each other? And above all, if they came here, what was to stop me from going there?

I gave little thought to the practical questions, of course, which would have deterred a sensible man. Did I ask myself what they might do to me? How I might escape? Whether I could even reach the mainland? Not in the least. I was too desperate to leave, preferring even death to remaining. Perhaps I might come to civilized lands, or find another European ship to take me in. Or I might die. If so, my years of loneliness and misery would be over.

As I reflect on my long captivity, that last train of thought astonishes me most of all. I had spent endless hours to make myself safer; now at least part of me felt death would be a deliverance. I believe my mind had grown disturbed. What drove me to this? Perhaps the biggest factor was the simple lack of any other person to speak with, much less offer me another point of view. Changes in my sense of safety—from safety to fear, and going back and forth between these— also had their impact. But the greatest factor was the sight of the Spanish ship, hanging lifeless on the shoal. This had raised my hopes, then slammed them down again.

How close I had come to companionship, only to miss out! Since finding the footprint, I had been disconcerted but mostly sensible. When I climbed aboard the shipwreck, only to find two corpses and a few tools rather than living people, I think my longtime loneliness finally boiled over in frustration. Something certainly boiled over in my mind, for this whole line of thought stirred my pulse up as though I had a fever. Imagine great anger without anyone to be angry at, or great love without anyone to lavish it on.

Whether through mental exhaustion or for some other reason, I drifted off into a deep sleep. One might imagine that I would have a dream of escape from the island, but this one was quite different.

I dreamt it was morning, and I was going out from my castle. I saw two canoes paddled onto the beach by eleven natives. As they landed, I saw another native in one of the canoes, destined to become a feast. The moment the canoes hit shore, though, the expected victim jumped out and disappeared into the woods. He came to my grove, seeking shelter, and I revealed my presence. I dreamed of smiling down to him, and that he seemed to kneel and ask for my help, whereupon I brought him into my castle. As my sleepy reverie continued, the native became a friend to me, and I thought: "Now I can certainly reach the mainland, for he will know how to get there, and will help me steer away from danger. He will know where to find food, and what places to avoid."

With that thought, I awoke. I went from a joyful dream back to dreary reality, and back into my depressed state. Was I going mad after all these years? In a way, perhaps. But this dream gave me an idea: I should try and befriend a native, ideally a prisoner about to be eaten, who could give me company and guidance.

But how? I would have to kill a whole troop, and I was uneager to do that even if it was the price of escape. I went through all the same sorts of internal disputes I have detailed for you earlier. In the end, and after much pondering, I decided to do whatever I must to get off the island—distasteful though my acts might be. I would begin to watch the shore again, and look for my opportunity.

For over a year and a half I kept going out to watch, both at the west end and the southwest corner of the island: nothing. This time, though, my frame of mind was different. The longer I went without result, the more eager I became. I didn't give up my watches; instead I grew careless with my concealment and noises.

After that year and a half of watching and waiting, I got a surprise one morning: no less than five canoes on shore together. I couldn't yet see the people who had brought them, but it was enough to man five canoes: at least twenty and maybe more. I had no idea how to attack twenty or thirty men single-handedly, and I stayed in my castle in full defensive posture.

After waiting and listening for a long time, I

grew very impatient. I set my guns at the foot of my ladder and climbed carefully up my hill, making sure not to show myself. With my spyglass I saw that no less than thirty people, with a fire going and meat dressed. They were all dancing around the fire, making wild gestures and motions.

As I watched, several men dragged two miserable wretches from the boats. A burly native struck one down immediately with a club or a wooden sword, and the victim fell stunned or dead—not that it mattered much, for two or three others immediately began cutting him open for cooking. The other was left by himself until they were ready for him. In that very moment, though, Nature inspired him with hopes of life. Seeing his chance, he took off at incredible speed across the beach, straight toward my castle.

I was frightened when I saw this, and more so when the whole pack of angry diners seemingly gave chase. Now it appeared that my dream would come true, and that he would certainly shelter in my grove; but I couldn't count on that. His former captors might pursue him here. I kept a careful eye on the chase where those involved revealed themselves, and grew hopeful when I saw that only three men were still after him. He was outdistancing even these, as well a man might who must run or lose his life. I guessed that he would lose them entirely, provided he

could keep going for another half hour.

Between them and my castle lay the creek where I had landed my first cargoes. The fugitive must swim it or be captured, and I couldn't know how well he would manage. My worries were nothing, for he made short work of the swim even with the tide high. When his pursuers reached the creek, two could swim but one looked at the others and turned back—a decision that saved his life, though he couldn't possibly have known it. The remaining two were superb swimmers, and the chase resumed on my side of the creek.

Now was my chance. Clearly Heaven had guided the fugitive in my direction, furnishing me means, motive, and opportunity to save his life. I ran back down to my castle, fetched two guns, hung a cutlass at my belt, and moved to intercept the chase. From my position that was a very short run.

I stood between the pursuers and the pursued, much closer to the pursuers. There was a general moment of shock all around. The fleeing man looked back at me in great wonder, and I beckoned him to return. I was afraid to fire a gun unless I must, for fear of attracting the rest with noise and smoke, so I advanced and swung my musket butt-first at the closest man. A solid hit in the side of his head: he fell senseless, perhaps never to rise again.

Now the second tracker halted and unslung a bow. At this range, he couldn't possibly miss if he got the chance to shoot; now it was the gun or nothing. I fired first, a bullet in his chest; he fell and lay still. Later I realized we were probably too far from the beach for my shot to alert anyone else, but for now I was quite nervous about it.

The fleeing native had stopped, but showed no inclination to come near. If I had never heard or seen a gun go off, I might not have either. I beckoned some more, but he came very cautiously. Later, I learned his reason: he thought he had exchanged one form of capture for another, new and more terrifying. I made every encouraging sign I could think of, and every ten or twelve steps he knelt down as if to thank me and ask mercy. When he reached my location, he did a very curious thing: he laid his head on the ground, kissed it, then set my foot on his neck. This, as I later learned, was his people's way of swearing service to another.

I encouraged him to stand; I smiled and tried not to look threatening. But there was more work yet to do, for the native I had clubbed down began to stir. I pointed to him, and my rescued companion said something: the first sound of another man's voice I had heard for over twenty-five years. There was no time for me to reflect upon that special moment, for the stricken man would soon be on his feet.

The man I'd rescued seemed afraid and about to run, but I pointed my other musket at his enemy. Seeing this, my man gestured urgently for my cutlass, bright and sharp at my belt. I handed it over, and he leaped and slashed without a moment's hesitation. No skilled executioner could have cut a man's head off as cleanly, and it made me wonder how he had learned such deft swordplay. Much later, I asked him about this, and his explanation was simple. His people made very heavy, hard wooden swords. These were sharp enough that a skilled wielder could cut off heads and arms with well-struck blows.

For now, my survivor laughed. He picked up the severed head, made a number of gestures I didn't understand, and laid both cutlass and grisly trophy at my feet. But he seemed very curious about the other man's sudden death, and I gestured him to go look. I saw great wonder in his eyes, for the mortal wound was a small hole in the chest, without much blood.

Whatever he thought of this, he quickly took up the fallen men's bows and arrows. I gestured that we should keep moving, in case of further pursuit, but my new companion made signs suggesting that he bury the bodies in the sand first. I signed agreement, and it took my man very little time to scrape and fill two shallow graves. I seem to recall it taking perhaps a quarter of an hour. I reloaded and stood watch, but no one else came.

When the evidence was concealed to his satisfaction, I led him away: not to my castle, but to my arsenal cave. Thus my dream did not quite exactly come to pass. Once in shelter, I gave him bread and raisins to eat, as well as a drink of water after his long run. Next I showed him to a place where I had laid some rice straw and a blanket, so that he could sleep, and he was exhausted enough to do so.

I looked him over during his rest. He was a tall, strong, handsome fellow, perhaps in his mid-twenties. His features were manly, but not fierce or surly; his smile had been quite handsome, his eyes bright and intelligent. His hair was long, black, and straight. His skin was not as dark as that of the Negroes of Africa, nor of the yellow hue common to Brazilian and Virginian natives; it was a sort-of dark olive. He had a round face, a small nose, and thin lips; his teeth were well-set, white as ivory.

After about a half hour of rest, he woke up and came out of the cave to find me milking goats. Again he ran over, laid down and placed my foot on his neck, making many unfamiliar gestures. The gist of these, which he later confirmed for me, was that he was very grateful and wished to offer me his service. I signaled that I was very pleased with him, and soon I began to speak to him. The day I had saved his life happened to be Friday, and I taught him this as his name. I taught him to call me "Robinson," then to understand and say "yes" and "no." I gave him some milk and bread, which I tried first to show him were good, and he ate and drank heartily. I decided we should bed down here, in case of pursuit, and go to my castle the next morning.

As soon as it was day, I motioned Friday to come with me. I indicated that I would give him clothes like mine, for he was quite naked—perhaps his captors had stolen his own. When we passed the shallow graves, he made motions suggesting that we should dig them up and eat them. I said, "No!" many times in great anger, pretended to vomit, and firmly beckoned him to move along.

I led him to my hilltop, gesturing for caution, so we could check on our enemies. The canoes were all missing, so it was safe to assume they had left. If they mounted any search for their lost prisoner and comrades, it must not have been extensive. I wasn't satisfied and felt we must investigate more carefully, so I gave Friday the sword to go with his bow and arrows. I had him carry a spare gun, and I took two myself. Thus well armed, down we went to the fire-pit area, to see what we might see.

On arrival, my very blood ran chill in my veins. The sight horrified me, though Friday seemed undisturbed. The beach was strewn with human bones, flesh, and blood, all mixed up. Three skulls confirmed what Friday told me using signs: they had brought four prisoners here to feast upon, and the other three had suffered this fate. He explained, as best he could, that the captives had been taken in a great battle between two tribes. These four prisoners were just a few of many taken from Friday's side.

The task sickened me, so I had Friday gather all the remains in a heap, whereupon we built a great fire and burned them to ashes. I could tell that he was still inclined toward cannibalism, but he was a very perceptive man. He made sure I knew he had no intention to actually eat any human flesh. From my earlier outburst, perhaps he suspected I would kill him if he tried.

When this disgusting task was finished, I brought him back to our castle—formerly my castle—and gave him some clothing. I had found some pants in the gunner's chest, and I made him a goatskin jacket to go with them. I had become a fairly good clothes maker and hatter in my years of practice, and I gave him a rabbit-skin cap as well. He seemed pleased to dress as I did, though he found the clothing awkward and chafing at first. After I made some alterations, he soon grew more comfortable in them.

Where would I lodge him, I wondered? I didn't yet fully trust him. I had been by myself for a very, very long time, and I was shy of others. At the same time, he didn't deserve to be banished to the woods. I decided to build him a little tent between my outer and inner fortifications, and I finally constructed a door for my cave entrance. At night I barred this and took up the ladders, so that he could not get at me without making a lot of noise. I kept all the weapons on my side. He didn't seem to mind any of this, and he thanked me for his tent in clear sign language.

All of this was a great waste of energy and worry, for no man ever had a more faithful and true companion. Friday did all that I asked of him, and he showed his sincerity in so many ways that I soon dispensed with precautions and set him up a bed inside my castle. I could see that he was making every effort to earn my trust, and he surely deserved it.

How interesting, I thought, that God had placed so many human beings outside the regions of His worship, yet endowed them all with the same powers of reason, affection, kindness, obligation, and all other human qualities and failings. I looked back on the natives I had met here and in Africa, who had often shown themselves better than Christians in many ways. This was true of Friday, though he had not the least knowledge of God in any Christian sense. In any case, I mustn't question divine judgment. Friday was here, and a loyal companion, and I ought to thank God for him and treat him well.

I began to teach him everything I could: work tasks, the English language, and where to find things. I was delighted with him, and more so as he began to learn my language. In fact, I may say that he learned more quickly than many children in England learn their lessons. He radiated good humor. All he wanted was to be helpful, and to do things well. I began to say to myself that if it weren't for fear of Friday's captors, I might not care if I ever left this island.

CHAPTER 14

Friday's Education

After we had been back at the castle for a few days, I felt it urgent to start educating Friday against cannibalism. I wondered how difficult this might be. Were I among Hindus of Asia, for example, they might well try to teach me not to eat beef from cattle—and they would have a very hard time. I saw no alternative, for I simply couldn't tolerate this practice. I wondered how I might make human flesh seem foul, and then I thought that perhaps I could make other food seem better. My boiled goat with broth would be a delicious start.

So I took Friday down to the pasture with me one morning. We never arrived, for on the way I saw that we wouldn't need to slaughter a tame goat. I saw a wild nanny lying down in the shade with two young kids beside her. Friday reached for his bow, but here was the chance to teach him something else. I caught him by the shoulder and had him wait, then raised my musket and shot one of the kids. The rest of the family went on a terrified romp to safety.

I didn't anticipate the effect on poor Friday. For the second time, he had seen me mysteriously kill at a distance with a great noise and cloud of smoke. He trembled in amazement, feeling his chest for a hole. I believe he thought his last hour had come, for he came and kneeled down to me, begging me not to kill him. I felt pretty bad about it.

How could I convince him he was safe? I gave him a hand up, laughed and pointed that he should go get the slain goat. Meanwhile I reloaded. He marveled at the kid's mortal wound while I scanned the trees. By-and-by I pointed out a great seagull to him, then pointed to my gun, and gestured that he shouldn't worry. I took good aim and fired, bringing the gull down. I pointed that he should go get it, and when he brought it back he seemed impressed and relieved—yet still a bit frightened. Well he might be, for he had yet to learn how the gun worked. To him it seemed a destructive power that must be placated, lest it unleash itself. For several days he would occasionally speak to it in the same tones and phrases he had used when begging me for his life.

That same evening I skinned and dressed the kid, then boiled the meat for our dinner. He ate the meat and broth with me, and seemed to enjoy it, but he looked shocked that I put salt on mine. He signed to me that salt was bad to eat, going so far as to put some into his mouth and spit it out, then rinse his mouth with fresh water. I put some saltless meat into my own mouth, and pretended to spit as if it were bad, but here I could not sway him. He never wanted salt in his meat or broth, at least not for a great while, and even then only a little.

The next day I wanted to feast him on roast kid. I hung it over the fire on a string suspended between two poles, turning it occasionally. Friday admired my method very much, but he liked the result even better. As our meal wound down, he told me as best he could that he was swearing off man's flesh. He surely wanted my approval, and I gave him every sign of it as I served him another helping.

Next I taught him to pound and sift barley. In this, as in everything, he learned swiftly. Time and again I was impressed at his quickness in the uptake. He only had to watch the process a time or two before he learned to bake bread as well as I could do myself.

With two mouths to feed, I felt I must farm more barley and rice. Here again I was impressed, for Friday was a willing, cheerful worker. He immediately understood that he was the reason for the extra work, and he showed that he was happy to help. All I had to do was show him the methods.

This was my happiest year yet on the island. Friday began to talk pretty well, with a good vocabulary of names for places and things. I actually had to relearn the art of conversation. I enjoyed our chats, but most of all I enjoyed just having him nearby. He was honest, direct, and friendly, and I grew very fond of him. For his part, I think he grew fonder of me than he had ever been of anything in his life.

One time I asked how he had been captured, and by now he had enough English to answer almost any question intelligibly (if not exactly in the King's English). It sounded like this:

Crusoe: Friday, does your nation usually do well in battle?

Friday: Yes, yes, we always fight the better.

Crusoe: If you always fight the better, how were you taken prisoner?

Friday: My nation beat then, too.

Crusoe: If your nation won, how could you be captured?

Friday: They many more than my nation, in the place where me was; they take one, two, three, and me. My nation overbeat them in the yonder place, where me no was; there my nation take one, two, great thousand.

Crusoe: But why did not your side recover you from your enemies, then?

Friday: They run, one, two, three, and me, and make go in the canoe; my nation have no canoe that time.

Crusoe: Well, Friday, what does your nation do with captives? Do they carry them away and eat them?

Friday: Yes, my nation eat mans too; eat all up.

Crusoe: Do they bring them here?

Friday: Yes, yes, they come here; come other else place.

Crusoe: Have you been here with them?

Friday: Yes, I have been here. (He pointed to the northwest side of the island, which it seems was his tribe's preferred side.)

So my companion had visited in the past, on the same sort of business for which his captors had in turn brought him. I took him with me to that side of the island. He recognized the place, and told me that one time they had come here and eaten twenty men, two women, and one child; he could not count to twenty in English, but he laid that number of stones in a row.

I asked him how far it was from our island to the shore, and whether canoes were often lost. He explained that it was very safe. A little way out to sea, he said, there was a current and a wind, always one way in the morning and the other in the afternoon. I thought at the time he meant the tides, but later I learned that it was the great draft and reflux of the mighty Orinoco River, for our island lay just off its many mouths.

From his description, I learned that his land was just across the strait from the great isle of Trinidad, north of the nearest river mouth. I asked Friday a thousand questions about the country, its people, the sea, the coast, and what nations were near; he told me all in complete openness. He told me that his people were called "Caribs," which meant that Europe knew them as the Caribbees, which our maps place on the South American coast from the Orinoco to Guiana.

He added that "a great way beyond the moon"—by this he meant beyond the setting of the moon, thus west—there were bearded white men like me, and they had "killed much mans." Surely he meant the Spaniards, whose cruelties in

America were a dreadful legend throughout the world.

"Could I reach these white men?" I asked.

"Yes, yes, you may go in two canoe." With some difficulty, he helped me understand what he meant here: a large boat the size of two canoes. He might help me to escape from the island!

It certainly wouldn't be the last time the thought occurred to me.

As time went on, I tried to share my religious knowledge with Friday. "Who made you?" I asked him one day.

"My father," he answered, as if it were a strange question.

"But who made the sea, and the land, and the hills and woods?"

His eyes lit with understanding. "Benamuckee, who lived beyond all."

"Tell me of Benamuckee," I asked.

"He is old, much older than sea or land. Older than the moon and stars."

"Why then, Friday," I inquired, "doesn't everyone worship him?"

"All things say O to him," answered Friday in grave tones. "Say O" was his term for praying.

"What of people who die in this country? Do they go anyplace?"

"Yes, all go to Benamuckee."

"Even those who are eaten?"

"Yes."

I began to instruct him in the God of the Bible. I explained that He was Maker of all things, and could do anything. The notion of Jesus being sent to redeem us seemed to appeal very much to Friday's sense of nobility and sacrifice. That He could hear us way up in Heaven also impressed my friend very much. One day he told me: "If God can hear us up beyond the sun, He must be greater. Benamuckee lives short way off, but he cannot hear until we go up to mountains to speak him."

"Did you ever go?" I asked.

"No. Only the old men, the Oowakakee. They go to say O, and come tells us what Benamuckee said."

"So they are your clergy, that is, men who help you in contact with what you cannot see."

"Yes. Clergy," he repeated, quite clearly. Odd indeed: the custom of priestly secrets was held in common between some forms of Christianity and these pagans. I wondered how some Christian priests would like hearing that.

"It's a fraud, Friday. These old men probably control your people's actions through what they report to you. They never come back to you and say that Benamuckee told them they have done wrong, do they?"

"No, they do not," he answered, taking my point.

I found it rather harder to teach him about

Satan, for his people had no such concept. "Well, as God is all-powerful, and encourages us to do right, the devil does the opposite. He tempts us to do wrong, and is God's enemy in all things."

"Well," says Friday, "but you say God is so strong, so great; is He not much strong as the devil?"

"Yes, yes," said I. "God is stronger than the devil, and we pray to God to help us against his evil. We ask Him to help us resist temptation."

"But," said Friday, "if God much stronger, why God no kill the devil, so make him no more do wicked?" I was strangely surprised at this question, and floundered for an answer. As you know, I was hardly qualified to answer deep questions of theology. I pretended not to hear him, and began to talk about something else. "No, I want to understand," insisted Friday. "Why God no kill the devil?"

Finally I recovered somewhat. "God will punish him severely in the end. We will all be judged, and he will be judged harshest of all, to be cast into a pit of eternal fire."

"Not understand," answered my companion. "If this devil very evil, cause of all trouble, then why God not kill him long ago, and stop all evil? Cut off roots of bad tree, tree dies."

"You may as well ask me," said I, "why God does not kill you or me, when we do wicked things. We do them now and then, but we are preserved, so that we can repent and be pardoned."

Friday gave this some thought. "Well, well," said he with a smile, "that well. So you, I, devil, all do wicked. All repent, preserved, God pardon all."

The idea of the devil repenting was unacceptable, but I didn't know how to explain the reality. Quite confused, I created a diversion by getting up in a hurry as though I must do something. I asked Friday to go get something that was a long way off. While he was gone, I prayed to God for a way to explain the point.

When he came back after some time, I explained with sincerity if not with precise knowledge: "God sent our blessed Lord Jesus to call us to repent for our wrongs. He loved us enough to send his son; but he sent him as a man, not as an angel. Angels are spirits who serve God as demons serve the devil. Because a man was sent, humans may receive the forgiveness. Angels do no evil, and thus don't need forgiveness. The devil and his servants cannot gain it."

This whole process of Christianizing my friend showed me how little I really knew, for many of the most natural questions had never occurred to me. It inspired me to deepen my own reading of the Scriptures, and thus my own faith matured and grew. How thankful I was for Friday! All seemed to have been well ordered by divine guidance. I was even thankful for having been cast away here to begin with.

In our three years together, I may say that Friday become a much better Christian than I. His questions were sincere and perceptive. When taught something, he would apply it to his life in ways I had not considered, and thus I learned to amend some of my own sinful thoughts and habits. Those were very happy years.

His English never grew quite perfect, but he certainly learned to communicate well. I told him about my own history, at least the part that had led to my shipwreck. I explained to him the mystery of gunpowder and bullets, and taught him to shoot. To his delight, I gave him a knife and a belt, with a hook to hang a hatchet. He understood that he had gained my complete trust, and he repaid it in a thousand ways.

I described England and Europe to him: how we lived, how we worshipped, how our society operated, and how English ships traded in all parts of the world. I showed him the place where the remnants of our ship—now long since broken and sunk—had rested in the shallows. I showed him the ruins of our old boat, which had fallen apart years before. Friday stood and thought for awhile, then said, "Such boat come to my nation."

"What do you mean by that?" I asked.

"Boat like this. It came on shore in my

country, pushed by bad weather."

"Perhaps it was a European boat," I mused aloud. I hadn't yet thought about whether it might have contained men, which was really quite dense of me. "What did it look like?"

Friday gave a clear enough description of the boat, but I understood him better when he added, "We save the white mans from drown."

"Were there any white mans in the boat?" I asked.

"Yes," he said, "the boat full of white mans."

"How many?"

He counted on his fingers. "Seventeen."

"What became of them?" I pressed.

"They live at my nation."

This put my mind quite full of thoughts. Might these be survivors from the Spanish ship? I had a surge of concern. "And what became of them?"

"They there about four years," he explained. "We at peace, give them food, no harm."

"Why, if you normally kill and eat people, did you not eat them?"

"We make brother with them," said Friday. "Only eat mans when caught in war." This was reassuring. It also sparked hopes and thoughts that would not die down.

Some considerable time later, on a long walk, we came to the hill from which I had once seen the mainland on a very clear day. Today was another such day, and Friday gazed intently that direction. Then he began jumping and dancing, calling out to me. I had been investigating an unfamiliar plant, and came over to see. "What's the matter?" I asked.

"Oh, joy!" said he. "Oh, glad! There see my country, there my nation!" I saw a sparkle in his eyes, and it was obvious that he longed for home.

This disconcerted me. I began to think that if Friday got home, he would not only forget all about his new religion but also about me. If he told his people about me, they might come back in great numbers, to make a jolly feast of me.

What a foolish, paranoid line of thinking! It wronged Friday very much, and to my embarrassment, I began to show these feelings. I was less familiar and kind to him, and he was far too intelligent not to see the change. He was fairer to me in this time than I deserved, applying the principles of Christianity and patient friendship all along. During this jealous phase, I often dropped hints or questions to see if he was leaning toward the subjects of my silly paranoia. Not a bit; his every motive was honest and innocent. He was perfectly comfortable, as well he might be, for he had done no wrong. I couldn't say the same.

One day, walking up the same hill, the day was too hazy for us to see the mainland. I asked him: "Friday, wouldn't you like to be back in your own country?"

"Yes," he said, "I be much O glad to be at my own nation."

"What would you do there?" said I. "Would you go back to eating human flesh? Would you turn your back on God's teachings, and follow these old men of Benamuckee?"

He looked grave and shook his head. "No, no, Friday tell them to live good. Pray God, eat bread and goat flesh, milk; no eat man again."

"Why, then," said I to him, "they will kill you."

He looked graver still. "No, no, they no kill me, they willing love learn. They learn much of bearded mans who come in boat."

"Would you go back to them?" I asked.

"Too far me swim," he said with a laugh.

"I'll make you a canoe."

His expression was thoughtful. "Yes, I go, if you come with me," he said at length.

"Won't they eat me?" I asked.

"No, no," says he, "me not let them. Me make them much love you, tell them you saved my life. They do with you like other bearded man, make free, give food, not hurt you."

Now I wanted all the more to meet these "bearded men," likely Spaniards and Portuguese. Maybe together we could get back to European settlement.

After some days, I took Friday to see my second canoe in its hiding place. "I will give you a boat to go back to your own nation," I said. We boarded it, and I learned that he was an excellent sailor. "Well, now, Friday, shall we go to your nation?" I asked.

He looked glum. "Too small."

"I have a bigger boat," I said, and we went there. Unfortunately, I had not looked at it for many years. It had lain so long it had split and rotted.

"Boat like this would do well," he said. "If not broken. Would carry enough meat, drink, bread."

So it would. We would simply have to build it.

CHAPTER 15

Rescue of Prisoners

*B*y now, I was dead set on going over to the continent with Friday. When I told him we would build him a canoe capable of the trip, he looked very grave and sad.

"What's the matter?" I asked him.

"Why you angry mad with Friday? What me done?" he replied in hurt tones.

"I'm not angry with you!" I protested.

"No angry! No angry?" said he. "Then why you send Friday away?"

"Friday, didn't you say that you wanted to be home?" asked I, now baffled.

"Yes, yes," he said. "Wish we both there, no Friday without Robinson." Ah—he would not think of going without me.

"What would I do there?"

"You do much good," he answered. "You teach wild mans good, pray God, live new life."

I would have chuckled, but I feared it might

hurt his feelings. "Friday, my friend, you don't realize. I'm no scholar or teacher. My people would say that I knew very little."

"You teach me good, so you teach them good," he insisted.

"No, Friday. You should go without me, and leave me to live here alone, as before."

At that, Friday did an odd thing. He jumped up, ran and got a hatchet, and put it into my hands.

"What in the world is this for?" I asked.

"You take kill Friday," he answered.

My eyes grew wide. I asked: "Why would I do such an insane thing?"

"Take kill Friday," he insisted, with tears in his eyes. "No send away."

Could any man be unmoved by such affection and loyalty? I set the hatchet down. "Friday, I give you my word: I will never send you away unless you ask to go."

I could see from Friday's expression that I had quieted his worry. His desire for home was based on his love for his people, and a desire to teach them what he had learned. As usual with Friday, it was far more unselfish than anything in my own mind. I wanted to find the marooned men, in hopes they might help me get back to civilization. As to taking Friday back to England with me, I hadn't really thought it through.

We set out to make a canoe large enough to

handle the trip. This time I certainly wanted to build it near water, but this time I also had Friday's technical expertise based on many centuries of handed-down wisdom. Add to that his muscle, and you can see where our options were greatly expanded. He selected a certain kind of tree, explaining why it was preferable; I wouldn't have guessed. Once we felled it, Friday showed me how to burn the cavity out in a uniform, careful, neat way; while we guided this, I showed him how to use axes to shape the outside into a boat. In only a month our canoe was done.

Then came the process of moving it down to the water. We had to cut great rollers. We would set them in place, heave, move the rollers, and begin again. It was another two weeks' exhausting work, but the reward was marvelous. The canoe we launched was perfect in every way, and would have carried twenty men with ease. Friday proved a most adept pilot during her trials. "Could we go over in her?" I asked him.

"Yes," he said. "We could go over, unless meet great wind." What he didn't know was that I meant to add a mast and sail, as well as an anchor and cable. The mast was easy to cut from a straight cedar tree; the sail was another matter. I had plenty of old sails, or pieces thereof, but I hadn't preserved them very carefully. Shortsighted of me, but then again I did not really imagine I would ever again have reason to hoist them on a mast. Most of them were indeed rotten, but I found a couple of pieces in pretty good shape. My sail making resulted in a very ugly three-cornered thing, what we call in England a "shoulder-of-mutton" sail, with the long side of the triangle stretching from top of mast to the canoe's bow. Trained sail makers would have laughed themselves silly at the sight, but it would carry us.

My rigging work took a couple of months, for I added a couple of smaller sails as well as a rudder. With all this done, I now had to teach Friday the art of sailing. He could paddle a canoe as well as anyone, but he was amazed what the rudder and sail could do. I taught him how to work these, and when one would furl or hoist various sails. The only matter of seamanship I could not get him to understand was the compass, but that didn't worry me. Fogs and cloudy weather were rare enough in these parts, except during the rainy season, at which time we wouldn't be at sea.

I now began my twenty-seventh year in captivity, though the last three years really ought not to count due to their wholly different character. I kept the anniversary of my landing here with all the same gratitude as before, but this one had a major difference: it might well be my last. Despite this sense of coming rescue, I kept up my work: digging, planting, fencing, gathering and curing grapes, and so on. With Friday, of course, it all proceeded faster and more agreeably.

Soon came the rainy season, and we stowed our craft as securely as we could. At the same place I had long before landed my rafts, we dug a little dock together. It was just big enough for our canoe, and once we got the vessel moored, we dammed up behind it and built a protective cover out of many tree boughs. This would keep our vessel in good shape until November and December.

As the weather began to clear, I started the process of gathering supplies for our trip. Within a couple of weeks, I expected we would be able to cut away the dam and launch our boat. One morning I was working at this, and called to Friday. "Would you please go down to shore," I asked him, "and see if you can find us a turtle and some eggs for our supplies?" We did this about once a week, so it was not a strange request, and away he went.

He hadn't been gone long when he came running back, fairly flying over my outer wall. Before I could speak he cried out: "Robinson! Robinson! Sorrow! Bad!"

"What's the matter, Friday?" I asked.

"Yonder there," he said. "One, two, three canoes!"

At first I thought he meant there were six, but soon he clarified that he meant only three. "Don't be frightened, Friday. We're well armed and they cannot see us," I pointed out. It didn't help; he was sure they were here to hunt him down and eat him. "Remember that I'm in as much danger as you," I added, "but that we can fight them. Are you ready to do that?"

"Me shoot, but there come many great number," said he.

"That won't be a problem" was my answer. "The guns will scare away those we don't shoot. Here is the real question, Friday: will you defend me, as I will defend you, and stand by me in battle?"

He nodded firmly. "Me die when you say." We each had a drink of rum, which I had carefully husbanded over the years, and then we began to make ready. I loaded the two bird guns with heavy shot, then loaded four muskets with two slugs and five small shot each. These weapons I divided evenly between us. I hung my cutlass by my side, and gave Friday his hatchet. We certainly would not be easy pickings.

When we were well armed, I took my spyglass up the hill for a look. What I saw just about made me sick on the spot.

I counted twenty-one natives with two prisoners, obviously preparing a horrid feast. They had landed not where Friday had made his desperate bid for liberty, but nearer to my creek—in territory I considered mine. I was doubly offended as I climbed back down to Friday, who had mostly gotten over his initial fright. "I'm going down there and put an end to this. Will you stand by me?"

"I die when you say," he answered without hesitation. I believe he meant that we faced certain doom, but that he didn't mind as long as he was at my side. Well enough. To our existing weapons I added a pair of pistols, one apiece. I had Friday carry the bag of spare ammunition.

When we were ready to move out, I gave instructions: "Now, keep close behind me, and after this be very quiet. Don't do anything until I say, and most especially don't start shooting until I give the word." We crept quietly through the woods, my goal to get as close as possible before opening fire.

On the way, however, I had second thoughts. I wasn't afraid of the visitors, for even alone I had them outgunned. With Friday I could overwhelm them. Rather, it was the same thought as before: was this right? Had I the right to play executioner? Perhaps Friday might; his people were at war with them, and if the tables were turned they would surely not spare him. To me, however, they had done no harm. I would go near, and watch, and then act as I felt God directed. I could resolve no further until I knew more.

We soon came near the edge of the woods. I sent Friday up a great tree for a better look, and he came down with a whispered explanation.

They were all seated about a fire, eating one of their prisoners, with another lying bound on the sand nearby—the next victim. He was not of Friday's nation, though no doubt he had been captured in some raid or battle involving that country, for my companion recognized him as one of the bearded men his people had helped. I went to the tree myself and saw that it was true: a bearded European lay bound hand and foot, wearing European clothes. There could be no question. I felt my anger rising to fury.

Just then, I saw a better place of concealment about fifty yards nearer. This would put us about eighty yards out, well within range and slightly above our targets. As we took our positions, I saw that there was no time to lose. Two of the visitors had been sent to butcher the other prisoner, and they were bending down to untie him. "Now, Friday," I hissed, "do exactly as I do."

"Yes." He took up a position on my right. I set down one musket and the bird gun, gently, and Friday did the same.

"I'll fire at those on the left. You shoot at those on the right. Are you ready?" I asked.

"Ready," he whispered.

"Then open fire!" I commanded, and with that I pulled the trigger.

Friday took much better aim than I. His first shot killed two, and wounded three more; for my part, I killed one and wounded two. They all went into a dreadful confusion at the sudden thundering *booms*; all who were unhurt leaped to their feet, but had no idea where to run or look, for none had spotted the muzzle blasts. Friday now watched me for our next move, and when I took up the bird gun he did likewise. "Ready?" I asked. He nodded. "Then in the name of God, fire again!" said I, letting off a blast into their confused group. Friday followed suit. While only two fell, many were wounded, and these ran about or writhed on the ground, screaming and bleeding. Soon three more fell down.

"Now, Friday," said I, laying down the empty piece and taking up the remaining loaded musket, "follow me." I rushed out of the forest so they could see me, with my brave companion close behind. When they spotted me, I shouted as loud as I could. Friday echoed me. We hurried toward the poor victim, whose prospective butchers had fled into a canoe with the first shot. Three others had managed to get into the boat with them. Everyone else was dead, or badly wounded, or shaking on the ground in terror, or had run off.

We could not, however, let the canoe's terrified paddlers return home to tell the tale. "Shoot those men!" I bade Friday, and he took good aim at the canoe. At first I thought he had killed them all, for his shot brought them all down in a heap in their boat. Two of them rose, wounded, and with no other directions Friday reloaded before they could make much progress. A second shot left no one visible above the canoe side, much less paddling. The scene in that boat must have been a horror, but it could not be a greater one than the carnage on the beach.

While Friday was taking his shots at the canoe, I drew my knife and cut loose the poor victim. Lifting him to his feet, I tried to remember my Portuguese. "Where are you from?" I asked.

"Soy Español," he answered weakly. Too bad I had never learned much Spanish, but I knew that much. I gave him a drink from my bottle and a piece of bread, and sent Friday back for the empty weapons. Thanks to the similarity between Portuguese and Spanish, I understood the gist of his next words: "Thank you very much, señor, for saving me!"

"Señor," I said in a great hurry, "we will talk afterwards, but now we must fight. If you can, take this pistol and sword. Some of them may recover."

He went to work right away with the weapons. The living natives were either trying to board canoes, or had run along the beach. I kept my pistol in reserve in case one of our side found himself in great danger, and worked to reload the muskets Friday brought. Relieved of these, my man joined the Spaniard in hunting down the remainder. The second phase of the fight was on.

One great fellow gave our Spaniard a good fight with a heavy wooden sword, but the European finally got through the man's guard with a mortal stroke. Meanwhile Friday accounted for most of the rest with his hatchet. One wounded man managed to swim out to the canoe Friday had blasted. A couple of the men had summoned strength to paddle it a little, hunching down. My companion fired twice more at them, but made no hits.

"We must chase in canoe!" said Friday. "They warn others!"

"Right you are!" I said. "Let's go!" I leaped into the nearest canoe, but it contained a surprise: a third unfortunate tied up in its bottom, just as the Spaniard had been. Small wonder he was paralyzed with fright, hearing all the commotion but unable to even rise up and see the cause. I immediately cut his bonds, and would have helped him up, but he lay nearly still. Most likely he had been bound a long time, and probably believed we were preparing him for slaughter. In much pain he rolled over, and I saw now that he was not European, but native. "Friday," I called out, "there's another man here. Come and see if you can understand his language."

My friend hurried over. Imagine my shock when Friday embraced the man, crying, laughing and shouting for joy! He sang and danced like a demented creature. It was a good while before I could get an explanation from him, but finally he shouted in English: "My father! This my father!"

It is hard to express how moved I was, watching Friday first embrace his father, then rub his arms and ankles to help restore blood flow. Gone were all thoughts of giving chase to the fleeing canoe, but we later learned that we were lucky we hadn't tried. Not long after they got out of our sight, a mighty wind came up and blew fiercely all night. Friday did not think they could possibly have ridden it out, much less reached their home territory.

But back to Friday. When he started to calm down, I called him to me, and he came leaping and laughing. "Your father surely must be hungry. Here." I proffered a handful of raisins from a pouch at my belt, and he gave them all to his father. Then he ran off as though bewitched, faster than I'd ever seen him go. He was out of sight before I could say much, and fifteen minutes later he came back carrying an earthen pot of fresh water along with some barley cakes. These we all shared, favoring the Spaniard and Friday's father, for they were both in sore need. We helped both men to comfortable positions, and helped them to massage away the stiffness of long bondage.

My poor companion! Every few minutes, no matter what he was doing, he would turn and look at his father as if to reassure himself it was no dream. After about an hour, our rescued men were doing better, but neither was ready for a march through the woods. I had an idea: "Friday, let's load them back in the canoe and bring them around to the dock. From there it won't be so far, and if need be we can carry them back to the castle." Between the two of us, we helped them aboard and maneuvered the boat along the coast to the river mouth. They still could not walk much, so I carried the Spaniard and Friday his father. It was tiring work, but in time we got them inside the castle.

As I helped Friday set up their temporary bedding, I reflected merrily that His Majesty now had a number of subjects. All owed me their lives; this was my land, and they were the newcomers. Somehow, I had managed to get subjects of three different religions: the Spaniard had to be a Catholic, Friday was a Protestant like myself, and his father was a Pagan. I decided that my lands should allow each man to believe as he chose, and left it at that.

Once my rescued prisoners were comfortable, I proclaimed a celebratory feast. I asked Friday to bring a yearling goat, and we built a fire to stew it. We dined together in joyful camaraderie, with Friday interpreting for all, for the Spaniard had learned the native tongue fairly well. What a delightful time of triumph and first encounters!

After dinner, I said to Friday: "Would you be so kind as to go bury the dead and their horrible feast?"

"Yes, bury all." He knew how much I hated any scene of cannibalism. I let our rescued men rest, and I cleaned up from dinner until my friend returned. At that point, in the cool of the evening, we picked up the discussion.

"Do you think the escaped men got away safely?" I asked Friday's father.

"They could not survive the storm," was the translated answer. "If they did, they were blown south, where other men eat them up. But even if survive and land safe, I think they not come back."

"Why not?" I had Friday ask.

"Not sure," came the answer. "Battle very noisy, like thunder and lightning, not like attack from men. To them you two—" he gestured at Friday and I—"like spirits come to destroy, not like men. I hear them all cry out this. They no idea how man can throw fire long distance, and speak in thunder. They never come back."

Later I learned the reality: a couple of the visitors had indeed survived, but they had told everyone that the island was haunted by terrible dangers and death sent by the gods. (I wondered what Benamuckee, or their tribe's equivalent, had to say about that.) Anyone coming to the haunted island would be destroyed with fire, or so the legend grew; but for now we couldn't know that. In mind of a retaliatory strike, I made sure we all kept on guard with weapons ready.

I had styled myself, half jokingly, a king; now I was one in fact. And the king now had an army.

CHAPTER 16

Visit of Mutineers

When no more canoes showed up for a while, I stopped worrying about them, and went back to my former thoughts of a voyage to the mainland. Father and Friday alike agreed that their people would receive me kindly. As glad as I was, I also had to consider the implications of the Spaniard's story.

His little colony consisted of sixteen Spaniards and Portuguese. The natives treated them well, but that didn't mean they were living comfortably. Their ship had sailed with a cargo of hides and silver from the Rio de la Plata in South America, destination Havana. They left their loading there and meant to bring back to South America what European goods they could find in Havana. They had saved five Portuguese seamen from another wreck, and lost five of their own when they had foundered on my island's shoal.

After a perilous voyage to the mainland, they made landfall in bleak condition: starving, with few arms and less ammunition, expecting a hostile reception. To make matters worse, they soon used up all their dry powder to hunt food. Now they were living off what they could find, or catch, or snare. The captain admitted that the nearby natives' charity was all that had kept them alive.

"Have you had any ideas about escaping?" I asked him.

"We talk mostly about that," Friday interpreted, "but our boat too leaky and no way to fix it. We had no tools to build another, no supplies. All our discussions fail, sad."

"What if I had an idea in that direction?" I had Friday ask. "Would your men consider it?"

"Sí, señor," said he in great earnest. Friday didn't understand that, but I did.

"I'll be perfectly honest with you," I said. "I am afraid to trust my fate to you. Your country forbids Englishmen to come here, and you have that dreadful Inquisition. I am a Christian, but not a Catholic. I don't want to be put in irons as a heretic, and I would rather be eaten alive than convert my faith. I could lose property, freedom, even my life! I can see a way we might reach either Brazil or the Spanish lands northwest of here, but only if you can assure me of my safety."

Friday's translation was very encouraging, if not grammatically perfect. "Señor," he said, "our misery great. Any man who help us, we do no harm. If you want, I go with you to ask old father of Friday, let him tell you how we are. My men swear by God and Bible obey you in everything. I now swear for me, loyal to you in all things. If my men break loyalty to you, I take your side. But they never do this. All honest men, polite, and suffering much. You come to help them, they stand by you like me."

"Then I shall," I said. "In the meantime, you must teach me Spanish, for I will clearly need to know it."

With all this arranged, Friday and I started preparing while our two rescued men recovered from their ordeal. Once the two new men were feeling better, we taught them to help with the regular farming and goatherding. I proved a very apt pupil in Spanish, probably because I already knew Portuguese, and within a month I could converse fairly well with my instructor.

When we had gotten together everything necessary for our voyage, the Spaniard raised a valid point. "Señor, perhaps we should wait half a year. While you have much food, your two new men have already put a strain on your supplies. You do not have enough for sixteen more, much less for a long voyage back to Christian lands."

His words made sense. "What do you propose?" I asked.

"I recommend that we wait," he replied,

"and the four of us farm the greatest crop you ever grew here. You have sailed, so you know that a food shortage can ruin the discipline of any group of men. Remember how the Scriptures tell us, señor, that the children of Israel were delivered from Egyptian captivity by God, yet when they grew hungry in the wilderness, they rebelled against God Himself."

"Well said, señor," I replied. "I have plenty of seed. Let us get to work."

We all went to work clearing, plowing, and planting every grain but what we must save for our own food in the meantime. I wanted more goats as well, so I organized some hunting trips to capture about twenty young kids. Our nannies more or less adopted these. The grape season came on, and never before had I hung so many. I believe we could have filled sixty or eighty barrels with the resulting raisins, the perfect food for sea voyages.

Our grain harvest wasn't as rich in quality as some I'd gotten, but it was surely my largest ever. We had planted twenty-two bushels of barley; we harvested two hundred twenty. From a somewhat lesser amount of rice we had also gotten a tenfold increase. When it was all threshed and stored, it would feed a crew for a trip anywhere in the Americas. We had to make many baskets to contain it, and to my joy, the Spaniard was very skilled in this.

With our food supply taken care of, I gave the

Spaniard my blessing to go over to the mainland and let his men know he still lived. "But here is my rule," I told him. "Any man who wishes to come here must swear, in your presence and that of Friday's father, to do no harm to me and obey my commands." Under these instructions, our two rescued men went away in one of the two native canoes we had captured, which Friday had recommended bringing around to safekeeping in the river mouth some months before. I gave each of them a musket, plus about eight reloads, urging them not to fire unless absolutely necessary.

This was cheerful work, taking my first solid measures toward deliverance in twenty-seven years. I gave them provisions of bread and raisins, hopefully enough to feed all the captain's men on a return voyage. We agreed on a signal they should hang out on their return, so we could tell them at a distance. They went away under a fair gale on the day of the full moon in October.

Eight days passed without sight of any vessel. On the morning of the ninth, Friday woke me up in great excitement, calling: "Robinson, Robinson! Someone come!" I jumped up, put on some clothes and wended my way past all my barriers with Friday on my flank. Down by the sea I saw something quite unexpected.

A longboat was headed ashore, with a shoulder-of-mutton sail like the ramshackle one I'd pieced together. The canoe we'd sent had no sail,

nor did native canoes in this region use sails. Did it contain friendlies or hostiles?

I had Friday keep watch while I went back for my spyglass, then headed to the hilltop. I took care to stay in cover. Now I could make out a second vessel well out to sea, and this was no longboat. It was a seagoing ship, built along English lines, apparently at anchor to the southeast.

I was full of more confusion and joy than I can express. These seemed to be my own countrymen, and probably friends—but I had doubts. English ships were rare in these waters; in Spanish eyes they were illegal smugglers, subject to boarding and confiscation. There had been no storms to drive them here in distress. If these were truly Englishmen, they might be the worst kind. If they were thieves and murderers, clearly I would be unwise to reveal myself. This hunch kept me on my guard.

Let no man reject the value of a hunch. I went back down to Friday's position, where we kept an eye on the longboat as it drew into shore not too far from my old dock. Now I could see by their clothing that the occupants were English, eleven in number. Three of them were hurried and prodded ashore with cutlasses: prisoners. One seemed to be begging for something, perhaps his life. Friday whispered: "Robinson, you see! English mans eat prisoner!" I think he found the idea more than a little ironic.

"No, no," I said. "I fear these Englishmen will murder these captives, but you can be sure they won't eat them." I was quite horrified, and more so when I saw one of the villains raise a great cutlass as if to slash the begging captive. Now I wished I had Friday's father and the Spaniard back, with us all armed. Luckily, the man with the cutlass was just intimidating the captives, and did not strike. Most of them fanned out and scattered, probably to look for fresh food. They put no guard on the captives, just a couple of men taking a nap in the boat; the three prisoners sat in a dejected group. I knew their despair well: in danger of attack by men or beasts, and with no hope of rescue.

We kept an eye on the area for a time, and I rejoiced to see that the tide was going out. In my experience, sailors never gave much thought for the future, and it seemed some things never changed. The water receded very far before one of the men in the boat awoke, saw the situation and yelled for the rest to come help him relaunch the boat.

Everyone came back and tried, with a great battery of curses and oaths, but it was too heavy for them to maneuver in the soft oozy sand. The seamen could not know when their boat would refloat, but I did: it would be ten hours. They scattered to their idle wanderings again, which I saw as a good chance to eavesdrop. Friday and I were used to the heat, but they weren't, and they would grow sluggish and inattentive.

In early afternoon, Friday and I fitted out for battle. I took myself two bird guns, and he carried three muskets, for I had to admit he was the better shot. If I chose to reveal myself, I would present a weird but formidable sight: dressed in goatskin coat and a great floppy cap, a cutlass and two pistols in my belt, and a gun on each shoulder.

By about two in the afternoon, they had all straggled into the woods for a shady nap. The three captives sat down beneath a great tree, seemingly out of sight of the rest. I thought this a wonderful opportunity, and Friday and I crept through the woods until we came very close.

I called aloud to them in Spanish, "What are you, señores?" They started up at the noise, but were ten times more stunned at my uncouth dress. Just when I thought they might flee, I spoke in English: "Gentlemen, don't be surprised. Perhaps I am an unexpected friend to you."

"Then Heaven must have sent you," said one of them gravely, taking off his hat to me. "Our condition is beyond any man's help."

"All help comes from Heaven, sir," I replied. "But maybe men are its agents. Surely you are captives, for I saw that man threaten you with his sword."

He trembled as tears ran down his face. "Am I talking to a real man, or an angel?" he asked.

"Sir, would God dress an angel this way?" I said with a laugh. "I'm an Englishman, and I mean you no harm. This man here is my friend and ally. You can see we are both armed. Can we help you?"

"It's a long story," he answered, "but I can tell you this much quickly. I was captain of that ship, and my men mutinied. Some wanted to murder me, but calmer voices won out—barely— and we are to be marooned here. They believe this island uninhabited. As for these two, one is my first mate, and the other a ship's passenger."

"Where did they all go?" I asked.

"Over in that thicket, sir," he answered. "If they hear us, they'll murder us all."

"Let them try. Have they any firearms?"

"Just two pistols, one of which they left in the boat."

I smiled. "Then you can leave that part to me, for as you can see, we have them very badly outgunned. It would be easy to kill them all, and if they have mutinied, the law allows this; but is it necessary?"

"Two of them are desperate villains," said the captain. "I would show those no mercy, for they will only cause you trouble. The rest, however, are followers. Kill those two ringleaders and the rest will return to their duty."

"Which are those?"

"I can point them out to you if we get near."

"Then let's get out of sight and earshot," I advised, "in case they wake up. We have matters to discuss." When we had gotten well into the woods, I gave this captain a level stare. "Sir, if I make the effort to save you three, I do so on two conditions."

"If you rescue us, I offer you the service of our ship," he replied, anticipating me. "If we aren't able to get it back, and we're stranded here, we will stand by you. Are those your conditions?"

"Nearly but not quite. Here they are," said I. "While you are on this island with me, you must not pretend to any authority. If I put weapons in your hands, you must be subject to my orders, and give them up when I say. Also, if the ship is recovered, you must swear to carry my man and me to England at no charge."

"I swear all of these things," he said in a sincere voice. "If you help us, I will never forget that I owe you my life."

"Well, then," I said, making up my mind, "here are three loaded muskets. Tell me what you think we should do." Each of our freed captives took a weapon.

"We should do whatever you say," said he.

"Very well. Then let's sneak up on them and shoot the ringleaders. If the rest fight back, we'll shoot them as well. If any surrender, we may show them mercy."

"Sir, I would hate to see most of them dead," he answered. "Except for those two low-lifes, the rest are decent men. If we let either of the ringleaders get back to the ship, they may bring back the rest to destroy us all."

"Very well. Let's get into position," said I. We worked our way to an ambush position. Soon the mutineers began to stir; three got to their feet, yawning and stretching. "Were any of those heads of the mutiny?" I whispered. The captain shook his head. "Then let's let them escape, so that we face a smaller number. Concentrate on the ringleaders."

The captain nodded grimly and checked his weapon. "Men, be ready to fire on my command, or if they spot us," he ordered in a hushed tone. As the remaining five mutineers began to stir, the former ship's passenger foolishly shifted position and made a rustling noise. A mutineer whirled about to look, saw us and cried out. At this moment two muskets cracked, with the captain wisely holding his fire.

It was a good volley, for one ringleader was killed on the spot—the man with the only pistol. The other was hurt but could get up. "Mates! Come help! We're ambushed!" he cried.

The captain ran forward and bashed him in the head with his musket. "It's too late to ask for help. You'd do better to pray God to forgive your crimes," said he. The mutineer probably didn't hear him, for he was either unconscious or dead; the rest stood quite still.

"Mercy, Captain!" they called out.

"I will spare you," said the captain, "if you swear to return to your duty and help me retake the ship, and sail her where I choose."

"We will! We will!" they assured him.

"Very well," said I, enjoying their stunned stares at Friday and myself. "But I do not trust so easily. While you are on the island, your captain will ensure you are bound hand and foot."

At once we stepped out with all guns at the ready. Three pairs of hands went up. "Don't shoot, cap'n!" they implored. "We know the game's up!"

"It is," he said coldly. "Now you must be tied up. If you help me get the ship back in its lawful hands, you will be spared. If you turn again, no mercy." They promised they would, and the captain took the other pistol from one of them. We had secured the entire party—a good job all around.

"Let's talk some more," I said to the captain, "for I have a good place we can do that. As for these men, we will secure them nearby where we can hear them. If they try to signal the ship, we will shoot every one of them."

"We'll do no such thing," said one who seemed to speak for all six. "We're at your mercy."

"See that you don't," I ordered. I led the party toward the castle, and we tied them all to trees well outside. "We will come back for you in time," I said, "but we're listening and we can see you. Try to escape, or cry out, and you'll be shot." All promised that they would do nothing of the kind. This done, Friday and I led the rescuees through the tangled woods and into our castle.

When we were all comfortable, I said to the

captain: "Now let me tell you who I am, and how I came to be here."

"By all means," he answered with a smile. I told the whole story of my life, from my reckless early days to the present.

"How lucky you were!" said he, when I was done. "To end up with food and weapons and ammunition, and to have survived so well! It's almost as if you were preserved so that you could one day save our lives!" He was deeply moved, and tears came; he could speak no more. I decided this was a good time for Friday and me to round up food and drink, and while our meal was cooking I showed our guests all my arrangements.

The captain was impressed most of all with my fortifications and concealment. "This is my castle and residence," I explained. "Like most princes, I have a country home as well. I can show you that another time; for now we must figure out how to recapture your ship."

"Agreed," said he. "But how? There are still twenty-six hands on board, and they know they face hanging. They will not surrender easily, and they have us outnumbered even if we can trust all our new captives."

"A good point," I observed. "We must split them up. Let's try to draw some of them ashore, so we don't have to fight them all at once. Surely at some point those on the ship will wonder what's become of the shore party, and come looking."

"They will," replied the captain, "and they will surely come better armed."

"Then let's prepare a surprise for them," I suggested. "After dinner, follow me down to their boat, and I'll show you."

They all ate dinner with great enjoyment, as did we, and then we took some water and left-overs to the bound captives. Next we released these from the trees and took them with us down to the beach, where nothing had changed. "What now?" asked the captain.

"Gather up everything useful out of the boat. Then hole it," I ordered.

"How badly?" asked the captain.

"Just make it unseaworthy, but nothing that we can't repair in half a day," said I.

We got some very good things out of the ship's boat: bottles of brandy and rum, some biscuits, a powder horn, and a great lump of sugar. I was delighted, for I had not had brandy or sugar for many years. We also took the boat's rudder, mast, sail, and oars and stashed them nearby. The captain made a neat job of breaking in a plank at the boat's waterline.

Most likely we would have another encounter with the mutineers. But if they simply sailed off, that also might work out well. With a little repair work, which the captain could supervise, we might call on our friends the Spaniards. We might even sail to Barbados.

Barbados, of course, was an English port. It was civilization.

CHAPTER 17

The Ship Recovered

*A*fter the captain disabled the boat, we untied the prisoners long enough for them to help us heave her above the tide line. When they were again secured, we took them into the woods and waited. Based on earlier consultation, we divided our captives into pairs: two the captain thought might turn on us, two he trusted, and two somewhere in between.

As evening approached, a cannon boomed from the ship. A signal flag appeared at her mast. "What does that mean?" I asked one of the prisoners.

"They say to get back on board," he said. The mutineers repeated their signal several times without answer, then began to hoist out another boat and row for shore. Through my spyglass I could see ten well-armed men aboard.

I gave the captain the glass. "Look over these men," said I, "and tell me what we can expect."

He watched for a bit. "Three of them are very honest fellows, who were probably forced into the mutiny. The scoundrel giving orders is the boatswain. The others are like him, but they're followers, not leaders. Under his command, they'll give us trouble."

"Not as much as we'll give them," I said. "Friday, you know of that small cave on the far side of the castle?" This was not my arsenal, but a smaller cave suitable only for shelter from sudden downpours.

"Yes. We got out of rain," he smiled. How fine to have one man I could absolutely depend on!

I pointed first to the former passenger: "Go with Friday and do as he says." Next I indicated the two least trustworthy men. "Friday, kindly take these two to that cave and secure them. Give them a little food and water, and tell them to stay quiet." I turned to the specified mutineers. "Disobey me," said I to the men, "and I will personally hunt you all down. I know every bush and rock of this place, and you do not."

"We won't, sir, we promise," said one. "We thanks you for the rations, and for treating us good." The other echoed this, and Friday and the passenger marched them away. The rest of us went back to watching the boat bear in.

"I fear they may overwhelm us," said the captain.

I smiled at him. "What happened to your

belief that we were put here to save your life? Never fear. The mutineers, except those who can atone, are about to be delivered into your hands. We are the last thing they expect. They don't realize it, but their lives are ours to take or spare."

Now I turned to the men the captain called honest. "If we release you two, do you swear to live and die by my commands?" They said they did, and I had them unbound and armed, for we had brought plenty of weapons. When Friday and his helper returned, we were seven honest men holding two captives. If the inbound mutineers could not depend on three of their number, the advantage of surprise should enable us to overwhelm them.

Soon, to my pleasure, the shore party ran their boat well onto land near the earlier craft. Had they instead anchored some distance out and waded in, we might have had a tough time. We kept silent as they all got out.

How surprised they were to find the first boat plundered and holed! They begin searching about, shouting and hallooing at the top of their lungs, all for nothing. I found it quite comical. Then they fired a volley of pistols. The only response they got was the one least expected: nothing. Not a sound. The gunfire echoed away, leaving only the sounds of surf and wind rustling through the trees.

Now they clustered together to argue over what should be done next. Later, they told us that the prevailing belief was that the first shore party must have been wiped out by natives; thus, they could do nothing but go back to the ship. All of them heaved until they got their boat back down to the water, then jumped in.

"Sir, we'll lose the ship!" whispered the captain.

Almost immediately, though, seven of the mutineers got back out and waded ashore, apparently as the result of further consultation. The other three took the boat a short way out to sea and anchored. The shore party began to move toward my hill in plain sight.

This was very bad news. While we could easily overwhelm the seven on shore, the rest would surely start out to sea in the boat. Those still aboard would have had enough losses from our island, and would surely sail off. All we could do was wait and watch. If they kept on, there was some chance they might blunder onto their two former fellows, but I never knew a sailor who liked long marches. This bunch didn't even climb my hill for a better view, but went up a short ways and began hallooing.

When that brought nothing, they sat down under a tree to discuss matters again. Too bad they didn't start to nap, as the others had done, or we would have taken them all without a shot.

Perhaps they were too nervous to sleep. Once upon a time, I certainly had been.

"They will probably fire another volley," the captain whispered. "Perhaps we should all rush in on them afterward. They can't possibly reload in time, and we'll capture them for certain."

"A good idea," said I, "provided they shoot." When they spent the time arguing instead, we had to rethink matters, and finally I spoke up. "It's getting toward nightfall. Most likely they'll go back to the boat. We might get between them and their friends in the boat, and come up with some tactic to get those latter back on shore."

Soon the men finished debating, got up, and headed for the beach. "Now they'll get away!" groused the captain. "What can we do?"

"Ye of little faith," I whispered back with a chuckle. "Doubting Thomas himself would be proud. Friday, take the captain's mate over toward the creek near the place where you were rescued, and halloo them at some distance. Do this until they answer you, and draw them inland, then loop back around to this spot. Keep hallooing as you approach, so we don't mistake you for them."

The searchers were just wading into the surf when Friday and the mate hallooed. With much splashing they ran back to the shore, then westward toward the voices. This brought them to the creek, which they couldn't easily cross at high tide, and they shouted for the boat. Soon the other three brought the boat well up the watercourse and threw a rope ashore. One of the boat's crew got out to tie the line to a tree and join the search. Just then, Friday and the mate came back to us.

Now I had them where I wanted them. "Excellent work, Friday," I whispered. "Now lead them to the remotest place you can think of, as far inland as possible and with no view out to sea. Get them lost if you can, and remember the spot; then come back. By that time we will have secured the boat and its guards."

Friday and the mate chuckled and left, hallooing as soon as they were well away from us. The eight searchers floundered off in pursuit, calling out names. Meanwhile I led my five men carefully to some woods near the mooring spot. I tasked the former passenger with watching the two men still bound.

When we came upon the boat, we found its guards completely unaware: one was sleeping on shore, the other dozing on board. "May I?" asked the captain, smiling in the evening light. "That one in the boat is one of the better men. I would spare him if I could."

"With a will!" I whispered.

The captain rushed forward with a clubbed musket. The man on shore stirred and turned just in time to see the musket butt whistling toward his forehead. *Thwack!* Down went the mutineer, sore and stunned but no worse. The rest of us secured him as the captain ran to the boat. Its only passenger had been napping, and now he rose to see what was the hubbub. He found himself staring down a gun barrel. "Surrender," the captain commanded, "or you're a dead man!"

"I strikes my colors, cap'n! I never wanted no mutinying to begin with!" said he, reaching his hands high.

"I doubt you did," said the captain. "Even so, Roberts, you have a lot to atone for."

"You can start by swearing your loyalty to me," I broke in. "Roberts, your captain has spoken up for you, which he hasn't done for this fellow." I shoved the other with my foot where he lay. "I take his word. Now give me yours."

"I swears, sir, I'll do as you says." Well he might, gazing into the barrels of several muskets, but fair enough. We untied the boat and hauled it to new moorings upstream where the outgoing tide would soon strand it, then told him to get ashore with us and wait. We tied up the other man, told him to keep silent if he wanted to live, and hid in the woods near the boat.

In the meantime, Friday and the mate led a marvelous wild-goose chase. Before long, the search party halted in confusion and exhaustion.

While the mutineers took time out to complain and grumble, our men came back to us, for it was near dark and they too were tired. By now the tide was well on its way out. A little bit later, probably by pure luck, the searchers found their way back to our direction. We could hear the ones in front calling to the rest to keep up, and those latter whining how tired they were.

What confusion when they showed up! Their comrades had vanished; their boat was stranded on the muddy creek bed, and not where they had left it. Now they began to speculate that they had come to an enchanted island full of ghosts and devils and spirits, and that they were all sure to be devoured. They called out for their two comrades many times without answer. Not even the boatswain showed much leadership, for he was the most dispirited of all. They all milled about, going from the boat to the shore and back. We had them almost where we wanted them.

My men wanted to attack at once, but I was loath to kill any without need, much less risk any of our own men. Our enemies were still well armed, and more desperate than ever. I resolved to wait, and see if they would separate further, so I had my party sneak up closer. I sent Friday and the captain off to one side, where there was more cover but only for a small number of men. "When you are as close as possible," I said, "you may open fire, and we'll follow."

They had not been in that spot for long when the boatswain came walking toward them with a couple of other men flanking him, thirty or forty yards from the rest. The sight of this hated enemy so near was too much for the captain. He stood up and fired, as did Friday, killing the boatswain on the spot and mortally wounding the next man. The third man made a run for it.

At the sound of musketry, I sent forward the rest of my force: the mate, the passenger, and the prisoners we had trusted with weapons. They advanced in the dark, very hard to see, and I had coached Roberts on what to say. Perhaps they might surrender without more fighting. Roberts called out as loud as he could to one of them: "Tom Smith! Tom Smith!"

A man immediately answered: "Is that Roberts?"

Roberts answered, "Aye, for God's sake, Tom Smith, throw down your arms and surrender, or you're all dead men."

"And who do we surrender to? Where are they?" asked Smith.

"Here they are," said Roberts. "Our captain and fifty armed men have been hunting you these past two hours. The boatswain is killed, Will Fry is wounded, and I am a prisoner. If you don't surrender, they'll shoot you all."

"Will they give us quarter, then?" said Tom Smith. "If so, we'll yield."

"I'll go and ask, if you promise to yield," said Roberts. He called to the captain: "Cap'n, will you give them quarter?"

The captain spoke. "If you all lay down your arms immediately, I'll spare you—all but Will Atkins."

From nearby, this Will Atkins cried out, "For God's sake, captain, give me quarter; what have I done? They have all been as bad as I!" This was a lie, of course, for the captain had told us it was Will Atkins who took hold of him during the mutiny. He had tied him very tightly, and bombarded him with curses and threats. I felt bound to honor the captain's choice in this.

"First you surrender," said the captain. "You can trust the governor's mercy, if he feels you deserve any."

At that, the whole band laid down their weapons and begged for their miserable lives. My men advanced to tie all their hands and hobble them. I kept out of sight for reasons of state.

Now we had to think of how we might retake the ship. One boat was holed but could be repaired; the other could not be used until the tide returned. In the meantime, the men pleaded with the captain. "Are ye takin' us back to hang, cap'n?" asked one.

"I ought to. You treated me villainously," answered the captain. "Surely most of you will eventually find your way to a rope no matter what. But as for now, you aren't precisely my prisoners. You thought you were marooning me on an uninhabited island, but in fact it has an English governor. He has the power to hang you here and now, if he chooses, or he may uphold the quarter I have given you. I suppose His Excellency will send you on to England—all except Atkins, whom I have been ordered to prepare for hanging in the morning."

Though the captain was of course making this up, I didn't mind, for it served my purposes. Atkins fell upon his knees to beg the captain to intercede with the governor for his life; and all the rest begged of him, invoking God's name, not to be sent to England. Our deliverance was at hand. It would take little effort to get these rascals to help retake the ship.

I whispered to the former passenger. "Tell the captain the governor has summoned him." He did as I said.

"Tell His Excellency I will come immediately," answered the captain, to reinforce their false impression of our numbers. When he arrived, I explained my view about seizing the ship. "Excellent," said he. "We can begin in the morning."

"Yes. But I want to be sure of success. We must divide these prisoners. Take Atkins and our bound men here to where the others are tied up; Friday will show you. The rest we will take to my country home, which is well fenced, and pen them in. In the morning, we will sort them all out."

This was all done, and with all our captives separated and secured, my army made camp at my country residence. I made sure none of the recent captives saw me.

It had been a very successful day. Twenty-one men had come ashore. Six were trustworthy in my service. Four of the worst were dead. Of the remaining eleven, five were close at hand, and six were confined elsewhere.

In the morning I sent the captain to try the captives confined within my fence, who had surely not had a comfortable night. I wanted him to assess whether they could be trusted to help recapture the ship, and listened at a distance.

"The governor has sent me to speak with you men," he began. "You have done me great wrong, broken the law of the sea. The governor has accepted your surrender for the present, but he can send you all to England if he chooses. Have no doubt that you will hang in chains there. If, however, you partially right your wrongs by aiding in the ship's recapture, I may be able to prevail on His Excellency to exercise his power of pardon."

Needless to say, they all swore that they would, with many oaths and promises, saying they would owe him their lives and think of him as a second father. Seamen in distress could be very dramatic.

The captain heard them all out, then gave his answer: "Well, I must tell the governor what you say, and see if His Excellency will agree." He came back to me, and said, "I believe they'll be faithful. They would probably swear to anything to save their lives, but they can do little else."

I thought for a moment. Then I said: "I don't want us to seem short of men. First go with Friday and bring the rest from the cave. When we have them all together, tell them that …" and I outlined a plan. The captain smiled and agreed.

The others were brought accordingly, and given some food and water. Only then were they brought into the presence of the rest. The captain asked: "Who wishes to help retake the ship and return to loyal service?"

"I do!" "I will, sir!" "Gladly!" came the chorus.

"Very well," said the officer. He named six names; Atkins was not among them. "Now, the other five of you must be accountable for your comrades. If any man shows bad faith, the five others will hang alive in chains on the shore, per His Excellency's orders."

Naturally, the captives began to implore their fellows, invoking old debts, friendships, and the name of the Almighty. When the captain was satisfied with the situation, he separated the five who would remain prisoners. Friday and the mate took them back to the small cave, left them some food and water, and untied their hands. The mate warned them as I had instructed him: "We will come to check on you, and keep you supplied with food and water. Each time, all of you had better be here, and still hobbled. Do anything else and His Excellency will carry out your death sentence." They of course promised to behave.

When Friday returned with the mate, the captain unbound his six choices. We had fourteen men we might arm, twelve if Friday and I stayed behind. Still I did not reveal myself to either the five captives or the six who had joined up, and I had decided to wait ashore for signals. Each of the six parolees was given a firearm, and we began to prepare for the expedition. The captain came in to report all this to me.

"Now, captain," said I, "if you're confident of your men, make ready. My assistant Friday and I will remain ashore to await your success."

"Right, Your Excellency," he said, playing the role to the hilt. "We must repair one boat and bring another around, and provision both of them. First mate, you will command one boat, and I the other, so take five men and get the boat from the river mouth while we repair the other."

Out they went to get the work going. The preparations didn't take long, but I told the captain not to make the attempt until well after dark.

When the boats left on their mission, Friday and I climbed my hilltop to watch for the approved signal of seven guns.

There was just enough moonlight for us to follow their progress. The actual details of course were reported to me later, but here is how it happened: the boarding party came within earshot of the ship, and had Roberts hail her: "We've found the men and the boat, but it took us a long time." He received a reply, and kept inventing details as both boats drew near. I had hoped darkness would hide inconvenient details, such as about half the original men being absent, and events bore out this hope. Soon our men were at the ship's side.

The remaining mutineers didn't learn that they were in trouble until the captain and his mate came up the side. The former second mate and carpenter, waiting for their "shipmates," were surely quite shocked to be struck down with musket butts. Over the railing came the loyal men. "Secure the main deck and quarter-deck!" ordered the captain. "Then the forecastle. Then we will go below and comb out the ship for every last mutineer." His men gave a hurrah, and the recapture was on!

The few others on deck quickly surrendered and were put under guard in the empty forecastle. Next was the roundhouse, and the captain ordered the first mate to break down its door and take it by storm. The mate attacked the door with a crowbar, but inside was bad news. The rebel captain had found two men and the ship's boy; they had managed to arm themselves and lie in wait. As soon as the door splintered, these mutineers fired.

A musket ball broke the mate's left arm, but even so he rushed the roundhouse with his men behind. He dropped his crowbar, drew a pistol and shot the mutineer captain straight through the head. The other three threw down their empty weapons to surrender. The rightful captain gave instructions to maintain a secure deck and lay his wounded mate down while he scoured the remainder of the ship.

Three more men surrendered without a fight in the cook room, and with that the ship was secure. It was a good fight, for we could easily have suffered worse casualties than one wounded.

Imagine my rejoicing to see and hear seven guns boom from the recaptured ship! Friday and I had waited until two in the morning for this. All my plans had been crowned with success, and now elation gave way to exhaustion. We fell asleep right there on the hilltop.

I awoke from sound slumber to the blast of a gun. I leaped up in surprise to hear a man calling out: "Governor! Governor!"

It was the captain, climbing to the hilltop and pointing to his ship. He was so overcome with emotion he embraced me, then said: "My dear friend and deliverer, there's your ship. She is at your disposal." I looked out to see the ship riding at anchor barely half a mile offshore, for they had moved her in near the creek mouth. The captain had brought a boat in near my old dock, so he had only a short walk.

It now dawned upon me. My own deliverance was at hand.

There could be no mistaking it. It was truly a ship, at my beck and call, ready to sail me wherever I asked. For some time I couldn't speak; I felt I might actually faint. The captain gave me a drink from a small bottle of fine cognac he had brought. Thus revived a bit, I sat down on the ground, still unable to say anything. The captain spoke many words of gratitude, all of which went in one ear and out the other.

Finally I broke down in tears, perhaps a summary of all the tears I had shed for loneliness and frustration. My hearty youth had passed away without a friend to talk to, a woman to love, or even a choice of where to be. It took me some time to recover the power of speech. My liberator simply put his arm about my shoulder; Friday, my dear friend, did the same from the other side.

When I could talk, I said: "Heaven sent you both: Friday as my friend and helper, and you, captain, as my deliverer. I can never again doubt the hand of the Divine. I must pray." I knelt and gave thanks, and as Christians, the others knelt with me.

When this was finished, I was somewhat myself again. "I've brought some gifts from the ship," said the captain, "at least what little those scurvy mutineers didn't plunder." He called aloud to his men in the boat, who began to carry a number of boxes and such our direction. We went down before the castle to meet them, and the bounty was marvelous: a case of French cognac, six large bottles of Madeira wine, two pounds of excellent tobacco, twelve good pieces of salted ship's beef, and six of pork. Also there were a bag of peas, a hundred pounds of biscuit in a barrel, a box of sugar, some flour, a bag of lemons, and two bottles of lime juice. I had not seen many of these luxuries for so long I just stared at them.

While I gaped like a fool, they brought forward the rest: six new shirts, six neck-cloths, two pair of gloves, a pair of shoes, a hat, a pair of socks, and a full suit of the captain's own clothing. Later on, I would find that I had great trouble getting comfortable again in European clothing, but it certainly looked inviting at the time.

After these ceremonies were past, and after these princely gifts were brought into my residence, we sat down to consider the remaining prisoners. "Should we take them along?" I asked.

"Two of them are absolutely worthless," said

he. "They will never reform. If we take them, it will be in irons, to be handed over to proper English justice."

"I believe that if I handle them correctly, they'll beg to stay here, and you won't have to worry about them," I answered.

"I would be very glad of that," said the captain.

"Well," said I, "Let's go and deal with it." First I dressed in my new clothes, which chafed and felt most awkward. I said nothing, of course, for it was a gift, and this was the result of many years in goatskin. I picked out two armed men as a safety precaution, and the captain and I went to the cave of confinement.

When we came near, the captain called out: "Stand for His Excellency the governor!" I heard rustling. All five men were still in place, looking frightened.

I let them see me for the first time, and I began to speak.

"I have now had the full story of your horrible mistreatment of the captain. You have stolen a ship, which is mutiny and piracy, and you were preparing to do further robberies. That is another hanging offense." I let them absorb that for a couple of seconds.

"But now you have reaped the bitter fruits of your evil," I continued. "Your ship has been recaptured. Your mutineer 'captain' hangs at the yard-arm." I led them to a nearby rise where they could see the ship, and the colors flying, and the body hanging limp and bloody.

"Now for you," I went on. "I have the full authority and power to hang you all as pirates caught in the act. Why shouldn't I?"

One seemed to speak for the rest. "Your Ex'llency, I can only say this. When we struck our colors, the cap'n promised us our lives. Now we ask Your Ex'llency's mercy. We done as ordered, and stayed right here."

"But what mercy might I show you?" I asked. "I have decided to leave the island with all my men. We are bound for England. If you come, you will be in irons, and at the first English port we visit you will be tried for mutiny and piracy. I need hardly tell you the penalty for that; you have all sailed past Execution Dock and seen pirates hanging. Tell me: just what mercy is possible, except for marooning you here?"

"Ex'llency, that would be more mercy than taking us back to Barbados or London," said the speaker. "Here we might survive. There we die like dogs."

"Well, if that's what you want, then I will confer with your captain and we shall return." As he and I went out of earshot, I could sense that he was angry.

"Those men should hang," he said, bitterly. "Alive they will never do good."

I grew testy myself. "They are my prisoners, not yours, and kindly don't forget it. I will not go back on my word. If you don't like them being set free here, you're welcome to hunt them down again."

"I could, perhaps, but I won't," he replied. "All the same, this leaves a bad taste in my mouth. Mutineers ought to hang."

"Then think of the effect on your other men," I argued. "Their mutiny was wrong, absolutely wrong. They treated you abominably. But if you now hang these five, or even some of them, the rest may wonder when their turn will come. Sparing them will not harm discipline, and leaving them keeps their mutinous voices off your ship."

I wasn't sure I fully convinced him, but he assented. Back we went to the captives, and the captain spoke. "I have yielded to His Excellency's wisdom. If you prefer to stay here, you may."

"Nor will we strand you without hope," I said. "I will leave you some weapons and ammunition, and teach you how you can live very well if you're willing to work."

They said they were, so I commanded them to wait there. The captain and I went back to the beach. "When would you like to depart?" asked he.

"Tomorrow, if you please," I replied. "I would like to take some last looks around, get some things to take with me. Will that be suitable?"

"Quite so," he said. "Signal us aboard when you're ready, and we'll send a boat for you." He left me alone with Friday.

Now I had my companion bring the men to my castle. "You made the right choice," said I. "You would surely have hanged otherwise. Now, if you will pay attention, Friday and I will teach you what to do. Listen well."

As we walked around the island, I told them my whole story. I shared my ways of making bread, planting grain, curing grapes, herding and milking goats, churning butter and ripening cheese. I also told them of the seventeen Spaniards, made them all promise to treat them well, and gave them a letter to deliver should the Spaniards visit. I also left them my weapons: five muskets, three bird guns, and three swords. Thanks to careful conservation, I could also leave them about a barrel and a half of powder. I cautioned them to plant rather than eat the bag of peas, and said I would ask the captain to leave them a few other supplies. I meant to try and coax from him some more powder, seeds for gardening, and other such useful things.

At last it was all done. There was nothing left to do but lie down for our last night of sleep on this island.

CHAPTER 18

Return to England

The next morning, with Friday's help, I loaded up the moldy, tarnished money from both wrecks. I took along my goatskin cap and my umbrella, and our work in this island was done. There was no question, of course, of leaving Friday—neither of us would have it. The captain informed me that we should delay another day to complete a few repairs, and of course I agreed. On the morning of departure, however, two of the five men came swimming to the ship's side.

"What are you doing here?" called the captain.

"Those others are bullying us something awful, cap'n," cried one of the swimmers. "We think they'll murder us to have more for themselves. For God's sake, sir, take us on board even if you hang us at the yardarm."

"I must consult the governor," responded the officer. Quietly I told him to do as he saw fit.

When he returned to the side, he addressed them again: "His Excellency says that if you come aboard, you must have a whipping and pickling, and then you must swear allegiance. Do you agree?"

"We do!" "Yes, sir!" they cried, and the captain ordered them hauled up. Each received ten lashes, followed by a splash of seawater, then promised his obedience. I talked the captain into leaving the marooned men some other supplies, plus their sea chests and clothes. Men strained to raise anchor; others went aloft to make sail. Sails filled with a perfect breeze.

Thus I left the island, December 19, 1686, the anniversary of my first escape from Sallee. I had stayed twenty-eight years, two months, and nineteen days.

After a long voyage with several stops, I arrived in England on June 11, 1687. I had not seen my native land in thirty-five years. It felt as foreign as China or Palestine.

First I went to see the lady to whom I had entrusted my money. She was alive, but had fallen on hard times in her widowhood. None of my money remained. In memory of her kindness, I forgave her what she owed me, and gave her some of the money I'd brought. I still owned property in Brazil, assuming there hadn't been some legal or physical disaster, and eventually I might be able to send her more.

What an interesting thing it was for Friday to ride in a carriage! "A canoe on land," was his comment as we went north toward Yorkshire. I had little family left, for my parents and brothers had passed on. Two sisters still lived in the area, as did two of my nephews. My parents' will had not included me, of course, as they believed me dead. Even so, it was wonderful to see my few remaining kin.

When we reached London again, our money situation got a small boost. The captain told the ship's owners that I was the driving force that saved their ship and most of its crew, and they invited me to meet with the ship's investors. In addition to warm thanks, they gave me almost two hundred pounds sterling; most helpful and much appreciated, but it would support us for a limited time. I must learn the status of my Brazilian estate, for which I must go to Portugal.

We reached Lisbon the following April, where I looked for my old friend and rescuer the Portuguese captain. He had now grown old and retired from the sea, and his son now operated the ship on the Brazil trade. After some time he remembered me, and we had a joyful reunion.

After we shared some old memories, I asked him about my Brazilian lands. He hadn't been there for about nine years, he said; both my trustees had passed away, but my partner was still living. In his view, under Portuguese law, I most likely had a fair sum of money coming. I owned half the plantation and its profits—up to a point. I asked him to explain.

From my date of departure to the time I had been declared legally dead, it was the duty of the trustees' heirs to account for my share. Of that my friend felt sure. Once the king's representatives decided I was never coming back, they would most likely have split my share between the King of Portugal and the monastery of St. Augustine. The latter would use it for relief of the poor and conversion of the Indians to Catholicism, and it might be gone; the former might not easily let go of a single coin. However, I might still have valid claim on these profits.

"Will I have difficulty asserting my claim?" I asked my old friend.

"Mostly not," he replied. "I am sure the king's men and the monastery have taken care to collect their shares. But that process began six years after you were left, and took another four to complete. The survivors of your trustees are good honest men, and my son tells me your partner has taken fine care of the property with numerous improvements. He is now very rich." I might also be, had I not gone on an ill-fated slaving expedition like a ninny. My friend continued: "With your partner as witness to your identity, you should be able to claim all that is yours."

"What was your role as my executor and

heir?" I asked, a little uneasily.

"Senhor, without proof of your death, I felt it unwise to take action. I could have pressed a claim on behalf of your estate, but that might stir up a great dispute. It would have looked like an effort to enrich myself. Once such trouble starts, it is difficult to end well. I preferred to hope you might return."

"I understand," I agreed after giving it a moment's thought.

"However," he went on, "I have other news for you as well, and some is not good. Your partner and trustees entrusted to me your share of the first six years' profits after you went missing, minus expenses; only then did the king's representatives consider your return a forlorn hope and begin legal proceedings to collect your profits. I do not know exactly how long that took, but it was done long ago. Thus, I owe you money or equivalent goods; your partner owes you an uncertain amount; the monastery and the state may owe you the rest, if they will pay. I will get my account book and tell you what I owe you in full."

He went and got the book, then shuffled until he found the place. "Here it is," he said. "That income, after expenses, was delivered to me in the form of four hundred and seventy moidores, sixty chests of sugar, and fifteen double rolls of tobacco." Moidores, of course, were

Portuguese gold coins. Before I could rejoice, he went on: "Unfortunately, I was shipwrecked with the cargo and lost it all, saving only the money. In my misfortune, I had to use it to cover my losses and buy a share in a new ship. But Senhor, I will see that you get what is justly yours."

"How is that possible?" I asked. I was sure my friend had every honest intention, but I couldn't eat honest intentions.

He got up to fetch an old bag, opened it, and counted out some money. "Here are one hundred and sixty moidores, and the title to my share in the ship, which comes to one-fourth. These I give as security for the rest of what I owe you."

I was too moved by the poor man's honesty and kindness to accept all of this. "Senhor," I said through my tears, "At your recommendation, I place my faith in the authorities and the others responsible. I can never forget all that you did for me. One hundred moidores shall I accept, and no more, and for those I will give you a receipt. I will repay you from the proceeds of my plantation. As for the title to your ship, I won't think of accepting it. If I get what is rightfully mine, then God has smiled upon me. If not, I will not press a claim upon you."

Now he could not hold back his own tears. "Senhor, you are a man of great honor and generosity. I will do all I can to help. Do you plan to go to Brazil to make your claim?"

"Must I?" I asked.

"You need not," he said. "The first step is to establish that you are legally alive. After that I will speak with a friend of mine, and we will begin the process." He had his carriage brought, and we traveled to the office of public registry. Here I affirmed under oath that I was Robinson Crusoe, and that I had rightfully gained ownership in the plantation. My friend swore and signed as well, and the necessary documents were prepared.

Next my friend wrote to a merchant he knew, explaining the situation and asking for his help. We would have to wait, of course, and the old captain opened his home to us until the matter was settled.

The next six or seven months were very pleasant, and at the end of that time I received a large packet from my trustees' survivors. When I sifted through it, I found that most matters had worked out well.

My trustees' successors were responsible for my share of the profits while the legal proceedings had plodded on, and they had sent them in the same vessel. Those came to two hundred chests of sugar, eight hundred rolls of tobacco, and several thousand moidores. The captain's merchant friend was glad to sell the goods for me.

The Prior of St. Augustine wrote to apologize that he could not get back what had been spent on the mission hospital and relief of the poor, but that nearly nine hundred moidores remained unspent if I wished to claim them. Not too surprisingly, the crown's taxing authority wrote to tell me that His Majesty owed me nothing, though I could claim my full future profits starting with the date of my return.

There was also a letter from my partner, rejoicing at my being alive, and giving a full history of the estate. He invited me to come soon and take possession of my property, or if I chose not, then to give orders for the delivery of my personal effects. As a present, he sent me seven fine leopard skins from a later voyage to Africa that had fared better than mine. In addition, he sent five chests of sweets produced from the plantation's sugar, plus a hundred gold moidores.

Try to imagine, if you will, the flutterings of my heart when I realized how wealthy I was. I now had more than five thousand pounds sterling, or rights to the same, if the moidores were exchanged. My estate in Brazil would produce perhaps a thousand pounds per year. I was rich—one of the few conditions in life I had never known.

My first act, of course, was to compensate my good friend. I showed him all the paperwork, and told him: "Second only to God's grace, you did the most to restore all this to me. Now I will reward you many times over." First I gave him back the hundred moidores. I sent for a notary, and drew up a document to formally forgive him all else he legally owed me. Then I had the clerk draw up papers empowering my friend as the receiver of the annual profits due me from my plantation. For holding these funds for me, the captain was to receive a hundred moidores per year for life, and his son fifty moidores a year for so long as he lived. How satisfying to feel that I had finally given him proper thanks!

Next I had some letters to write. I wrote to the Prior of St. Augustine, thanking him for his honest dealings and asking that the monastery give half my money to the poor, and use the rest for other good works. It would have been insulting to send a monetary gift to my trustees, but some gratitude was in order, so I wrote to thank them for their justice and honesty. As for the King of Portugal, I knew it would be very unwise to write His Majesty saying, "Thanks for nothing," and I let that matter go.

Lastly I wrote to my partner, returning his compliments and speaking well of the work he had done on the plantation. In the future, I asked that he entrust any sums due me to my old patron until I advised him otherwise. I told him I meant to come there and settle. To this I added a very handsome present of some Italian silks for his wife and two daughters, plus a few other European luxuries rare in the New World.

And now what? I was used to a very carefree life, with no worries about money. I had no cave to hide it in, nor any place to lock it up. Where should I put it? My only sure place of safekeeping was with my old friend the captain, and so much money would be a burden. I wanted to go back to Brazil, and see my property and friends, but I couldn't do that until I safeguarded my new wealth. The only other person I know of who might help was my old friend the widow. She was honest, but poor and in debt. Her creditors might seize her meager assets, and mine with them. It might take years of trouble to retrieve them—if I even could.

While taking some more months at the captain's to think this over, I decided it was time I did right by my friend the widow. First, through the captain's merchant friend, I sent her one hundred pounds with the promise of more later. I also sent each of my surviving sisters a hundred pounds, for one had been widowed and the other's husband was lazy and unkind. Well and good, but my problem remained: among all my relations I had no one to hold the rest of my money while I was away.

I saw no other real option but to take my wealth to England. Perhaps I could find a safe place of storage or a faithful custodian. I dawdled and hesitated; twice I booked passage, and once I even had my wealth loaded aboard a ship bound for London, but I changed my mind each time. And let no man doubt the value of intuition, for it was a good thing in both cases that I didn't sail. Algerian pirates captured the first ship; the other was lost in a Channel storm, with only three survivors. Had I taken either, of course, I would have lost all my money and perhaps my life.

My patron recommended that I go instead by land through Spain and France to Calais, then take a short voyage to Dover. Nor need Friday and I go alone, for he found an English gentleman willing to travel with me, and he knew two more English merchants who wished to join us. Two young Portuguese gentlemen wanted to go as far as Paris. I hired an English sailor as my servant, and with many fond farewells Friday and I left my dear friend the captain.

As I have spared you the dull details of my sea voyages, I will do likewise for my land journeys, except for some of our adventures. We spent some time seeing the sights of Madrid, but we came to regret the delay. Nearing the Pyrenees Mountains, we met some travelers who said that they were turned back by heavy snow in the passes. We tried to press on, but I had long become unused to any sort of winter at all. I feared I might lose fingers and toes to frost, and Friday had an even harder time with the cold. Afraid he might die outright from exposure and pneumonia, I decided we must return to Pamplona and await better weather.

Poor Friday! While there was shelter in

Pamplona, it was hardly enough for him. Never in his life had he seen snow, nor felt such icy winds. The roads were impassable, and everyone called it the worst winter on record.

Twenty days later, the weather hadn't improved. The only alternative to spending all winter in Pamplona was to sail around the mountains and resume our land journey at Bordeaux. Just as I was ready to arrange this trip, I met four French gentlemen who had just come through the passes with little trouble. Intrigued, I asked how they'd managed it.

"A helpful guide brought us, Monsieur," they answered. "He is still in Pamplona."

"Will you send for him?" I asked.

When the guide arrived, I asked him to tell me how he had succeeded where everyone else was failing. He said, "I know paths that are not as badly affected by the snows. I could lead you there, but you must be armed, for there are packs of starving wolves that direction."

"I fear the two-legged kind of wolves most of all," I explained, for there was much gossip in Pamplona about banditry in the mountains.

The guide smiled. "I know where those kind roam. We will steer well clear of them," he said. We agreed to follow him, as did some twelve other stranded gentlemen with their servants, and our expedition left on November 15.

I was quite surprised when our guide first led

us back toward Madrid, then north again by another way. The mountains looked dreadful, but he led us along a winding way that avoided nearly all the snow and steep slopes. Except for one brief halt to wait out a day and night of heavy snow, we made fine progress. As we descended toward the beautiful farms and fields of southern France, there was less cold and wind with every step.

Two hours before nightfall the day after the snowstorm, our guide was scouting ahead when three monstrous wolves charged out of the woods. Two made for our guide, who was barely in our sight. One wolf grabbed his horse's bridle and held; the other leaped up to attack the guide. He had not even time to draw his pistol.

Friday was riding alongside me, of course, and we spurred forward to help. Lucky for our guide Friday was along. He was used to such creatures in his country, and had no fear of them. While I halted to take aim at a safe distance, Friday was far braver and calmer. He simply rode up and shot the attacking wolf point-blank in the head. At the sudden blast, the other wolf let go and fled.

In that moment we heard the most dismal howling of wolves you can imagine, with the noise echoing off the mountainsides as though there were many dozens. Our guide was hurt, but not mortally, with a savage bite on the arm and another above the knee. But for Friday, the man would have been dragged from his mount and devoured. He was most grateful to my South American friend, as were we all, for without our guide we would have been in dire straits.

Not, of course, that all was yet well. A shuffling sound along the road made that perfectly clear.

CHAPTER 19

England—to Stay

*B*ears, of course, are wild and unpredictable. A mounted man might escape one, but on foot his survival generally depends on the bear's mood of the moment. There are very few in South America, and surely my friend had never seen one.

When this bear came rushing out of the woods, Friday and I had dismounted to tend our guide's wounds. The monster halted fifty yards away to look us over. Everyone was nervous but my companion, whose eyes shone with joy and courage. "Watch, Robinson," said he. "I invite him to dancing, make you all laugh. Please hold my horse."

"Don't be a fool," I said. "He'll eat you up!"

Friday laughed and pointed. "No, I eat him up!" Before I could protest, Friday borrowed the guide's gun and took off toward the bear. About twenty feet away, and to my great shock, he stopped and addressed the creature in his most formal English: "Wait a moment, good sir, I would like a word with you."

The bear just stood and stared at him. Perhaps offended at the lack of a civil reply, Friday threw a big rock at the bear's head. It did no damage, of course, but the bear gave a roar and charged. Friday laughed and came running back toward us—with the bear in hot pursuit!

We all got ready to shoot at the bear. "Fool!" I cried out. "Is this your idea of making us laugh? Get back here and mount up while we shoot him!"

"Don't shoot," said Friday. "Stay still, and you will have big laugh!" I am sure that the bear never saw a human being who could run like Friday, for I never had. Halfway to our position, he turned hard right and headed for a great oak tree. The bear moved to follow him with a great, frustrated roar.

Another of Friday's great skills was the ability to climb a tree almost as swiftly as a squirrel. My man laid his gun down at the foot of the oak tree and started up. The bear stopped, smelled the gun, decided it wasn't edible, and started up after Friday.

Bears of course are fine climbers, provided the tree can hold their weight. We all rode for the tree, not getting too close. Friday could not stop laughing as he climbed out onto a long, thick branch. The bear came along the branch, but at a certain point he sensed the limb would not hold his weight.

"Stay clear so we can shoot him!" I called to Friday.

"No, not shoot!" he called out. "More fun to come!" From his perch on the branch, my companion began to make the most amusing faces and grimaces. The bear bellowed his frustration.

Friday stood up on the limb, grasped a higher one, and began to swing back and forth. The bear began to claw off great chunks of bark from his tree limb in his fury. Next Friday swung over to an adjacent limb, and I saw his plan. The bear couldn't possibly follow him without clambering back to the trunk and onto a new branch.

From his new perch Friday called out: "Now, big monster, I teach you my people's dance!" And here Friday, with perfect balance, began to dance on the thick limb. We laughed until the tears came while the bear could only vent his anger on the air and the tree. "No, monster, you very slow learner. Also very impolite to your teacher, making so much noise. You should show more respect for wisdom of tribe elders." By now I think we were laughing too hard to even take good aim at the bear.

The great animal could perhaps leap down and survive, but a bear is no cat. Our monster was more or less stranded, and Friday moved effortlessly through the branches until he was able to leap down with ease. He retrieved his gun, gave me an elaborate imitation of a sailor's salute and mounted up. I was still too overcome with laughter to chide him for taking such insane risks. Even so, we didn't stop to give our guide's wounds better attention until we were at least a couple of miles past the bear.

The ground still had snow in places, and we

could hear wolves howl in the distance. We later learned that they did a lot of mischief among the horses and sheep that year. The howling chilled my heart, for it reminded me of the wild animal cries I had heard on the shores of Africa. On we rode.

Soon our guide advised us that we were coming to one of the more dangerous spots on the trail: an intermittent forest frequented by many wolf packs. As these would surely be hungry and desperate, he urged us all to keep a good watch. Ahead lay a narrow trail, then a forest, then the village where we were to lodge that night. Our guide, who was not a very bold fellow, stayed very close to the rest of us.

Half an hour before sunset, we came to the woods. Nothing appeared until we reached a large open space, where a pack of five big wolves tore across the road ahead as if chasing some prey. We halted and made ready, but they kept after whatever they sought and were soon out of sight. "There may be more," said our guide, and I sensed a tremor in his voice. "Be at the ready." I doubt any of us needed the encouragement.

Further into the clearing the ground began to level off, with woods still on all sides. At that point we saw a sign of trouble perhaps a hundred yards ahead: the body of a horse or mule, it was impossible to know which, picked clean to the bones. Perhaps a dozen wolves were gnawing away at the remnants. The guide led us around the grisly scene at a good distance, and the wolves stayed with the carcass. Friday wanted to try a shot, but I told him not to, for he might need all his loaded weapons sooner than he thought.

A hundred yards or so past the carcass, we heard a chorus of terrible howls from the woods on our left. Presently they came, almost in a line, like a disciplined force of cavalry with skilled officers and sergeants. The guide looked back to me, as organizer of the expedition, for orders.

I wasn't sure of the best way, but I knew one thing: any man who got separated from us would probably be dead in the next few minutes. "Wheel left and form line!" I commanded. "Remain close together. On my command, every other man shall fire his musket. The rest will fire when I call for the second volley. After that, draw your pistols and prepare for close action!" My party shifted and got ready, calming the skittish horses as the pack came on. Each man had one musket and two pistols, and most had already proved at some time or other that they could shoot. If all those were expended, we would have to resort to swords and long knives.

When the wolves were within easy musket range, I shouted: "First group—*fire!*" The muskets cracked, dropping four wolves and wounding some others. The rest hesitated but didn't retreat. I remembered something I'd been told long ago: even the fiercest creatures fear the voice of man. "Each man—give the loudest halloo your lungs can produce!" I ordered, and the whole company began to shout. The pack hesitated, began to back off. Now to put them to flight! "Second group—*fire!*" This volley killed fewer but routed the rest. "Reload," I commanded. "Then let's move on before they change their minds."

The pack wasn't long out of sight when we heard another terrible series of howls up ahead and on the left, punctuated by some other noises we couldn't identify. The ground was too rough for our horses to go faster than a trot. It grew dusky, which was very bad for our side, and in the declining light I saw shadowy forms moving on several sides. There were three troops of wolves: one on our left, one behind and one in our front, all keeping their distance. Our group kept close and pressed forward, watching in every direction.

Ahead of us the clearing began giving way to more woods. The pack in front had halted there in apparent confusion, and I wasn't sure whether we should wait or ride all the harder. Then from somewhere ahead came the *bang!* of a musket, and a saddled horse rushed out of the woods near the trail with more than a dozen wolves at his heels. We didn't interfere, as the chase didn't come near us, but I doubt that horse survived the night.

I supposed that we might go that direction to get around the wolf pack in our path, and the guide agreed. Entering the forest where the horse had emerged, we came on a hideous sight: one horse carcass and the bodies of two men, all terribly gnawed up, one with a gun laying next to him. The shot we had heard was likely his final act in life. I looked around to see the various packs of wolves beginning to edge closer, blocking every exit. Now we must stand and fight for our lives.

To our great good fortune, several trees of manageable size had been cut down in this area at some earlier date. "Drag them into a triangle!" I ordered. "And hurry!" When this crude defensive position was ready, I had the horses brought into the center and posted men all along each front. The wolves were closing in.

"We will fire as before, every other man," I called out. "Make sure of your targets! All servants stand ready to reload weapons!" When the wolves were in point-blank range, I gave the command: "First group—*fire muskets!*" Some fell to our volley, but the rest came on. "Second group fire muskets!" This volley killed more, and the rest began to hesitate on all sides. "All ready pistols!" I bellowed at the top of my lungs, then: "First group, *fire!*" Pistols cracked, sending heavy balls of lead into the flesh of many an attacker. After the second pistol volley, the marauders began to draw back a bit all around.

"All men to reload muskets!" I called. When my sailor-servant went to obey, I grasped his arm, saying: "I have a special mission for you instead. Take your powder horn and lay a good trail of powder all along the logs. All you men, stand back a bit from the logs!" Everyone obeyed in good order.

When the wolves regained courage and made their next charge, I stepped forward and fired off a pistol right next to the trail of powder. Loose powder doesn't explode, but it will of course burn, and a number of the wolves caught fire as they crossed our primitive walls. Those ran yelping in pain to roll around and put themselves out, and the few who didn't catch fire were put down with pistol shots at close range.

Seeing that the rest had got all the fight they could handle for one night, I ordered one last volley of every ready pistol. More wolves went down. "Now give another shout!" I called out, and my men all let go a great *"hurrrrrahh!"* The pack retreated, leaving many of their number dead or wounded. We came out of our perimeter to finish these off with swords. I could only hope it was done with, for we might not be so lucky if they struck again. Perhaps sixty wolves lay dead or badly wounded, and once all weapons were reloaded I gave the order to mount up and ride on.

The next hour was filled with frightful howls

from all directions, but no attacks. It began to snow, which reassured me that my desperate tactic wouldn't start a forest fire. After that hour's travel we came to our destination village, and the place was up in arms. The villagers told us that some bears and wolves had attacked their settlement the previous night. They were on constant watch to protect their lives and property. After such desperate battle, what a relief to bed down for the night in relative safety!

The next morning our guide was doing badly. Both of his wounds were infected, and he was feverish, so I paid him for his work and set him up in good lodging to recover. We engaged a new guide, and he took us to the city of Toulouse with its blessed and complete absence of snow, wolves, or anything else troublesome.

We told our story at an inn during our Toulouse layover, for inn patrons are usually eager for tales. I had thought I'd managed our defense rather well, but an old retired guide informed me otherwise. "What sort of guide did you hire, who brought you that way in such a season?" asked the old fellow. "You dismounted and put your horses all in the middle? Insanity! The horses were what the wolves wanted most. Had you stayed on the horses, the wolves would have feared you the more, because they don't understand that a mount and rider are two separate creatures. To them, the combination of horse and man means great danger. You did have one fine idea, though, I'll grant: that trick with the powder. They didn't expect to catch fire, and they won't run through much of it even if they're starving, as yours surely were."

"Well, I thank you for the information," said I. "For my part, I was never so terrified in my life. I believe I shall never cross those mountains again, even if it means sailing around in very stormy seas."

Nothing else exciting happened during the rest of our trip through France. Our young Portuguese gentlemen left us at Paris, and we headed north to Calais on the English Channel. The weather was cold, but bearably so, and there were plenty of towns to halt in. We landed safe and sound at Dover on January 14.

I was back in old England.

First I went to see the dear widow, who was most grateful for the money I had sent her. She offered to help me any way she could, and I would need that, for I had few contacts in England now. Friday and I stayed with her a time, and I reacquainted myself with all the comforts and ways of my homeland. Friday adjusted quite well, despite some strange looks now and then, and in time his English could hardly be told apart from a born Englishman's.

I decided to sell my interest in the plantation, so I wrote to my old friend in Lisbon. He felt that the trustees might be willing to buy it, and they responded to my inquiry in due time with a fair offer. I sold my interest to them 33,000 pieces of eight, which were remitted to their correspondent in Lisbon. I signed the bill of sale and sent it along. In good time my money arrived, minus the necessary amount to fulfill my annual promise of one hundred moidores to my friend and fifty to his son.

And thus a life of fortune and adventure was reduced to bankers' sums. I had begun foolishly, but my travels had ended up far better than I'd ever dared hope. I considered a return to Brazil, or other wanderings, but my friend the widow pleaded for me not to. This time I listened better than I had to my poor dead father's good sense so long ago.

Instead I took in my nephews, both partly grown. The eldest had inherited a bit of property and might do well managing it, so I raised him to be a gentleman. The other had a spirit of adventure like mine. Rather than implore him not to follow his wishes, I found him a berth with my good friend the ship captain. When my young relation proved sensible yet bold, I put up money for a ship of his own. Both grew into fine, prosperous fellows, devoted to their uncle.

I married, and had three children, but my wife passed on at an early age. With little else to do, I sat down with my old journals and combed my memories for the account you, dear reader, have nearly finished. All is revealed as best I can remember, withholding no detail despite the embarrassment it might bring me, for I did much to be ashamed of in my youth.

I can only hope that my old age may make up for it, and that my tale will let others share my adventure without leaving their sitting rooms— or if they find inspiration, that my lessons and trials may help them do well with God's grace.

In either case—fare you well!

Afterword

About the Author

Robinson Crusoe has been considered a classic of literature for centuries, and its author is often called "the father of the English-language novel." From these facts you might guess that the book's author had lived a dignified life filled with honor and respect. In fact, he was at times a fugitive, a prisoner, and a debtor, and a spy for hire. If he was admired for his writing, he was also despised for his political opinions and his willingness to work as a public relations person for the rich and influential.

The author of *Robinson Crusoe* was born in London, England, in about 1660. Surprisingly, his name was not Daniel Defoe. It was Daniel *Foe*, and he was the son of a butcher, James Foe, and his wife Alice. The Foes belonged to the Presbyterian Church in a time and place where the government openly favored the Church of England. Presbyterians were commonly known as "Dissenters," or people who opposed the majority opinion.

As a youngster, Daniel received very progressive schooling by the standards of his day. Instead of focusing on Latin and Greek, the Dissenters' school he attended concentrated on economics, science and modern languages. By 1683, he was doing reasonably well as a merchant, and he soon married Mary Tuffley, a young woman with a small fortune of her own. But like a true "dissenter," Daniel was not content to quietly go about his business and live comfortably. England had been torn by religious and political strife all Daniel's life, and in 1684 he joined a rebellion against King James II, England's last Catholic monarch. When the rebellion failed, Daniel had to go on the run to avoid landing in jail.

When it was safe to return home, Daniel went back to his business affairs. He was good at making money, but even better at spending it. To the end of his life, his story included burdensome debt, bankruptcy court, lawsuits from creditors, and new schemes to make money.

Sometime around 1695, Daniel changed his name from plain "Foe" to "Defoe," apparently to make himself sound more aristocratic. At about the same time, he began to write political pamphlets—a means of communication that was very popular. Daniel became the best-known pamphleteer of his day, gaining a broad range of

supporters and nearly as broad a range of enemies. In 1701, he published one of his most successful works: the poem *The True-Born
Englishman: A Satyr*, which scolded the English
for resenting the fact that England's King
William's was originally from Holland. The
poem, naturally, made him popular with the king,
and until he wrote *Robinson Crusoe* a generation
later, Daniel would be best known for this work.

But once again, Daniel didn't seem able to
quietly accept his good fortune and stop riling
people up. In 1703, he decided to criticize the
persecution of Dissenters. He wrote a pamphlet
in which he sarcastically proposed that all
Dissenters simply be put to death so as not to
cause any more bother. The authorities were not
amused. They hauled him into court on a long
list of charges which can be summed up as 'caus-
ing trouble.' He was sentenced to be pilloried—
that is, put on display with his hands and head
locked in a large wooden clamp. The idea was
that passersby could verbally abuse the prisoner,
as well as throw rotten fruit at him. But Daniel
acted quickly. As soon as he learned his sentence,
he wrote a poem called "A Hymn to the Pillory,"
which was widely distributed. When he was put
on display, then, the amused crowd that gathered
read his poem aloud, drank his health, and threw
flowers!

Although he got through his pillorying easily,
he was next sent to spend six months in the filthy

Newgate prison, a place that would make the worst modern jail in the U.S. look like a fancy country club. When Daniel later wrote of Crusoe's isolation, it's easy to imagine him drawing on the memory of lonely days in a squalid cell.

His six months in Newgate convinced him that he never wanted to go back. When Daniel got out of jail, he hired himself out to government officials to write pamphlets in support of their policies. It has recently been revealed that he also accepted money for spying on critics of the government. His actions had two obvious advantages: they kept him out of Newgate, and the money and powerful friends would keep some of his creditors at bay. He became increasingly well-known as a writer, but increasingly criticized as well. His critics called him a money-grubbing hack with no principles, while his supporters called him insightful and idealistic. One thing is clearly true: Throughout the early 1700s, Daniel became an increasingly versatile and polished writer. Along with his political writings, he produced histories, family advice and true stories.

In 1719, Daniel Defoe published *Robinson Crusoe*. The book was an instant success, and it went through six printings in only four months. What made this new work special was its *realism*. Instead of the poems and religious works that people were accustomed to, this book spoke in ordinary language about real places and real cultures. And yet *Crusoe* strayed far enough from the path of the ordinary to inspire readers' imaginations at a time when the English nation was sailing new seas and staking new claims. The public clamored for more, and Defoe wrote two sequels, but neither gained the acclaim or readership of the original book. In his usual fashion, Defoe managed to go through his earnings from *Crusoe* rapidly, and was soon beset again by debts.

When he died on April 24, 1731, Daniel Defoe didn't leave his heirs much other than unpaid bills. But he left the literary world a classic that would maintain its appeal for three centuries—the story you hold in your hands.

About the Book

*H*ave you ever visited a museum and seen a famous painting or piece of sculpture? Or maybe you've picked up a book or magazine and seen a reproduction of some masterpiece—the "Mona Lisa," perhaps, or Michaelangelo's statue of David. Chances are, your brain has registered "Famous art!" and you've stared at it for a minute, thought "That's pretty cool," and moved on.

But have you ever looked at such a work and reminded yourself that once, that was just a blank canvas, or a block of marble? At some point, a human being, an ordinary mortal with faults and flaws and good points and bad, looked at that blank surface or that hunk of rock and began slowly and painstakingly creating the work that we are familiar with today. A thousand little things influenced the final outcome. Think about it. Maybe if Leonardo da Vinci had cut himself shaving that morning, the "Mona Lisa" would have come out a little differently. If Michaelangelo had noticed a young man playing soccer as he walked to his studio one afternoon, perhaps he would have had a different model in his mind for David.

What does any of this have to do with *Robinson Crusoe*? The point is that when we regard a work that is regarded as a classic—something that has been praised for hundreds of years, and that we've been told again and again is excellent—it is easy to forget that it has not always existed. Nor did it somehow spring into existence, perfectly formed. It was once the laborious, time-consuming creation of an ordinary human being—perhaps one with great talent, but an ordinary mortal all the same. And it took the form it did for particular reasons. The "Mona Lisa," the "David," *Robinson Crusoe*—they all reflect their creators' personalities, faults, beliefs, and the times in which they lived.

In the case of *Robinson Crusoe*, author Daniel Defoe was influenced in his writing by at least three important factors. One was the stories of real-life castaways. The second was Defoe's beliefs about religious faith, sin and redemption. And the last was Defoe's acceptance of a widely accepted idea: that the British Empire had the right and duty to colonize the non-Western world.

A Real-Life Robinson Crusoe?

There were several stories of actual castaways circulating during Defoe's time. The best-known of them, and the one generally thought to have inspired Defoe, was the story of a Scotsman named Alexander Selkirk. The son of a shoemaker, Selkirk got in trouble with the law at age nineteen, and ran away to sea before his case could come to court. He became a "privateer"—that is, a sort of pirate who was licensed to raid ships belonging to the English king's enemies. In Selkirk's case, these enemies were Spanish ships off the coast of South America. Selkirk did well at sea, soon being offered the position as sailing master on a privateer called the *Cinque Ports*. But he soon regretted accepting the job. The captain of the ship was a tyrant, and after a few gun battles with the Spanish, Selkirk was seriously worried about the condition of the ship. His quarrels with his superior grew so heated that he finally demanded to be put ashore. His captain gladly obliged, leaving him on the uninhabited Juan Fernandez Island, far off the coast of Chile, in September 1704.

Selkirk took with him a gun, bullets, gun powder, a few carpenter tools, clothing and bedding, tobacco, a hatchet, and a Bible. He found a cave to live in, but became so terrified by his isolation and the strange noises he heard from the interior of the island that he spent months sitting on the beach, hunting for shellfish as he watched hopefully for a rescue ship. When sea lions finally drove him off the beach and into the island's interior, he discovered a lush area where he gradually taught himself to hunt and to domesticate the local goats. On February 1, 1709, when two British privateers dropped anchor at his island, the sailors were astonished to find "a wild man, something like a hairy ape," dressed in goatskins,

awaiting them. After four and a half years of solitude, Selkirk was unable to speak sensibly to his
rescuers for some hours. (By the way, Selkirk's
suspicions about the *Cinque Ports* turned out to
be well-founded. The ship had sunk off the coast
of Peru, and most of its crew had drowned. The
seven who survived, including the captain, were
captured and thrown into a Peruvian jail.)

Rather than hurry back home, Selkirk accepted a position on the ship that rescued him. It was-
n't until 1712 that he returned to Scotland,
astonishing his family and bringing with him a
small fortune. A year later he published an
account of his years on the deserted island, which
Defoe read. Incredibly, Selkirk still had not had
his fill of adventure. He went to sea again in 1720,
and died of yellow fever off the coast of Africa.

Defoe's Religious Vision

Although *Robinson Crusoe* is primarily thought of
as a great adventure novel, it is also a kind of
book that was very popular in Defoe's day: a
"spiritual autobiography." That is, the book tells
the story of the narrator's journey from sinfulness
to confession to redemption by a merciful God.
This theme is presented early. Young Robinson
Crusoe rejects the wise and loving counsel of his
father, and soon after that, he discounts the advice
of his first ship's captain. It seems clear that both

men are authority figures second only to God in Crusoe's life. By making Crusoe refuse to listen to them, Defoe is demonstrating that the young man is in rebellion against God and his will.

Crusoe continues in his arrogant, sinful ways, living an immoral sailor's life and giving no thought to God's will for his life. He suffers through shipwrecks and enslavement (which Defoe implies are punishment for his sins). When he is repeatedly saved and given a chance to redeem himself, he ignores God's efforts on his behalf and instead concentrates on making himself rich. (Although we see later that Defoe has no problem with a man becoming rich, he suggests that one should humble oneself before God and admit that the success is all his doing.)

Coincidences through *Robinson Crusoe* are Defoe's further hints that God's hand is involved everywhere. Crusoe notes that the date he ran away from home was the same date he was captured and made a slave. The date that he survived his first shipwreck was the same date he was cast ashore on the island, as well as being his birthday.

As the years go by, Crusoe is increasingly burdened by a sense of his own sin and aware of the power of God. With occasional setbacks, he begins to be sincerely thankful for what he sees as God's mercies in his life, such as providing him with seed to grow his grains. Although he never stops hoping to be rescued, he comes to see his soul's salvation as being more important that his physical deliverance from the island. When Friday comes into his life, one of Crusoe's dearest wishes is to convert his friend to the Christianity which he has come to depend upon. After his rescue, Crusoe finds his wealth not only intact but greatly increased—a reward, we infer, for his now Godly life.

Colonialism

A question might have occurred to you: "How can Robinson Crusoe be presented as a moral, religious man when he was involved in buying and selling slaves?"

It's a good question. Certainly for modern readers, there are few more appalling notions than the buying and selling of other human beings. But Daniel Defoe—and therefore his creation, Robison Crusoe—was a man of his time. A bit of background is useful.

In 1719, when *Robinson Crusoe* was published, England was a great colonial power, extending its empire through the globe. There was a popular saying, "The sun never sets on the British Empire" which suggests the expanse of Britain's power. In Defoe's time, it extended through such far-flung territories as Canada, Jamaica, India, Australia, New Zealand, Jamaica, and Barbados. Daniel Defoe had grown up surrounded by people who believed that

England had the right and the duty to occupy and "civilize" the rest of the world, particularly the non-Western portions. A important way that the British (as well as other Western powers) justified the practice of slavery was by saying that through slavery they could bring "the true religion"—Christianity—to natives of other lands, thereby saving their souls. Of course at the same time the colonizers were helping themselves to a tremendous source of cheap labor.

Once shipwrecked on "his" island, we see Crusoe's colonialist mindset in action. Although he works hard on the island, this is not man who started "from scratch." He has been fortunate enough to land on a natural paradise, rich with fruits and game. He immediately begins regarding himself as the island's proprietor and sets about improving his property. He imagines himself at various times to be its prince or its governor (as England habitually put English governors in power in the lands it was occupying).

It is in Crusoe's relationship to Friday, above all, that we see the colonizer's fantasy of how the world ought to work. Certainly the relationship is, as Defoe presents it, a pleasant one. Crusoe is undoubtedly fond of Friday and praises his intelligence, industry, and innate morality. But the bottom line is that Friday is Crusoe's slave, just as the men that Crusoe wanted to purchase in Brazil would have been. Can you imagine how different the scenario would have been if a white man, a fellow European, had washed up on the island? Crusoe and he would have interacted as peers, not as master and servant. If the white man had spoken a language other than English, Crusoe would undoubtedly have tried to learn the other language, as he had attempted to learn Portuguese and Spanish. The two would have pooled their resources and ideas for surviving and escaping the island. But with Friday, Crusoe is clearly in charge. Friday unhesitantly accepts Crusoe's leadership and instruction. (Remember, this is Defoe's fantasy!) He learns the white man's language, accepts his religion, and refuses to part with him, even when given the chance. As great a read as *Robinson Crusoe* is, it is also an uncomfortable reminder of how the slave-owning colonizer justified his world view.

Like any work of art, Robinson Crusoe does not exist in a vacuum. It is, in a sense, a mirror held up to its author and his world. A thoughtful reader can deepen his or her experience by having a sense of what that mirror reflects.